# FROM THI
## TO HIC

CW00618122

## B. H. Dawson

*Brian H. Dawson*

ARTHUR H. STOCKWELL LTD.
Torrs Park   Ilfracombe   Devon
*Established 1898*
*www.ahstockwell.co.uk*

*British Library Cataloguing-in-Publication Data.*
*A catalogue record for this book is available*
*from the British Library.*

*Arthur H. Stockwell Ltd., bear no responsibility*
*for the accuracy of events recorded in this book.*

In memory of my dear wife June (1931-2003).
Love always.

ISBN 0 7223 3618-7
*Printed in Great Britain by*
*Arthur H. Stockwell Ltd.*
*Torrs Park    Ilfracombe*
*Devon*

# Introduction

I was born in the small rural town of Whitchurch, Shropshire on 13th September 1934, on the outskirts of the town in a council house. I was the youngest child of seven children.

I would like to tell you about both my parents to make my story more interesting. Ladies first. Mum was born in the busy mill city of Bradford, Yorkshire, in 1897. She was the youngest of six children; two boys and four girls. Both boys died before reaching twenty with TB.

After leaving school she was trained as a seamstress and dressmaker, which came in very handy after she married as she made all our clothes when we were kids.

Mother did not have a very happy life, her own mother died when she was very young with cancer and her dad remarried — not a very nice woman by all accounts.

Mother was like a slave and was not allowed to kneel down but had to squat when she was working. Mother said she was pulled up by her plaits if her stepmother caught her kneeling. She had to black lead the grates and scrub the slate floors when she was very young.

Her father was a very religious man, turning to religion after his father drank all the family business away — I understand he had been a big mill owner in Bradford.

My grandfather's name was John Wood and to top it all he was a cabinet-maker by trade and he brought home offcuts of wood in his pockets and turned them out each night; that is what they had for toys.

The order of the day on Sundays was chapel three times a day, no Sunday dinner; home and back just for a cup of tea and a wash.

When Grandfather died Mum's stepmother went to Ceylon (Sri Lanka) as a missionary, and that is where all the family money went when she died. The family were not left a penny, the house had to be sold and that was it. Religion also rubbed off onto Mum and she practised what she preached; not just going to church or chapel on a Sunday to see Mrs Jones' new hat or 'Did you know so-so's daughter is having a baby and is not married' etc. I have gone to bed many times and seen my mum kneeling by the bed saying her prayers.

I never remember getting a smack when I was a child, but woe betide her sharp tongue. She would say things to you like "If you don't behave I'll knock the living daylights out of you." But it all boils down to respect really. When your parents say no it should mean no.

This should give you an idea of what sort of person Mum was, now for my dad.

Dad was the second son of seven boys; Walter, George, Joe, Bert, Bill, Ted and Fred. Bill had a twin sister but she died at birth. Dad was born in July 1894 in a red brick house called Bofia on the outskirts of the town in the hamlet of Broughall on the side of the main Whitchurch to Nantwich road.

My grandad, who I can remember quite well (the only grandparent I can remember), was Arthur Dawson who moved with his parents to Whitchurch from Bradford as a young boy in the early 19th century.

Great-grandad, as I understood, moved from Bradford to start up a foundry and agricultural business in the town with a W. H. Smith & Sons, a firm which was still running when we moved to Wales in 1951. Sadly it closed down in the mid 1960s. Four generations of the Dawson family had worked for the firm; Phillip being the last.

My grandmother was a farmer's daughter from The Meadows Farm, Ash, and farmed with her two unmarried brothers. Her maiden name was Pennill. When my grandparents married she left her two brothers on the farm (they never did marry).

I did not have a very good start to my early life. My mother told me that when I was only two years old, while waiting for my dad to come home from work I twisted my ankle as I stepped down from a small wicket (small gate). We went to Wind Cup holiday camp near Rhyl for a week's holiday the following day and while there my ankle started to swell. And after coming home from holiday Mother took me to the doctors in town but was told by the doctor to take me back in a week or so because it was too early to find the problem.

The following week the doctor told my mum to take me to the SOH at Gobowen (this was 26.9.1936. I found this out from my hospital records less than two years ago). Mother said a Sister Arthur put a plaster cast on my leg up to the knee. I loved Sister Arthur for many years, and she was still in the hospital plaster room up until the mid 1960s. My mother was told by the doctor to take me back to the hospital in six weeks time. He also told her that he thought I had got into the habit of limping. Mother told me I used to cry a lot because my leg hurt.

It seems it got worse as the weeks went by, and before the six weeks were up Phillip told my mum that my foot was smelling and that a discharge was running from my toes. Mother rushed me to the doctors and was then sent by car to the SOH.

As they were cutting the plaster off they found my leg had stuck to the plaster with it being on too long and my ankle had gone rotten inside the plaster. Mother told me it was horrible and when they finally got the plaster off they could not stop me screaming with pain.

This was the start of a very long stay in hospital to try to save my leg (around two years). A number of operations were performed on my ankle and it was touch and go whether I was to lose my leg.

As the weeks passed into months I started to know where I was but Mum and Dad were not able to visit me on the ward; they could only look at me through the windows. I was now being treated for TB and only nurses and staff were allowed onto the ward. I was in the babies' ward, (Wheatley Ward), the first ward on your right as you entered the hospital. Wheatley Ward was pulled down in 2002.

As I got older I was allowed visitors but only adults. Dad and Arthur used to cycle from Whitchurch to visit on a Saturday and Sunday. Mother would travel in the week on the old GWR train, changing at Oswestry for the old Oswestry to Gobowen line which ran every quarter of an hour; getting off at Park Hall Halt.

I cannot remember walking while in hospital, but we were in big cots with high sides which were pulled up with a loud clang. As I remember all cups and plates were aluminium and all battered and bent. We used to bang them together and shout "We want some more, we want some more, we, we, we, we, we want some more." I can't remember whether we did get some more but I can remember getting a smack off one of the nurses.

I must have been around four years old by now because I can remember a big rocking horse and doll's house we used to play with. The doll's house and rocking horse were there for years and I can see them now.

By now I had been fitted with an iron to the top of my leg known as a Thomases Splint which I wore until I was eleven years of age. From eleven until I left school I had a short iron to the knee.

In 1938 I was moved from SOH to a place called Gredington for convalescence for the summer. It was like a nudist camp, a very hot summer, I remember getting an all over tan.

The ward was I think a converted stable belonging to Lord Kenyon. I remember pheasants coming into the ward for crumbs etc., it was a lovely summer.

I went home for a year or so just when the war started.

I was back in the SOH again in 1940, on Ludlow Ward this time. This was the children's ward next to Wheatley boys' ward nearest the main road (the girls' ward next to the main entrance). Ludlow Ward is now a private ward.

I remember the hit song in 1940 was the Ink Spots singing

Why do they Whisper Green Grass.

I was in hospital this time to drain fluid off my ankle, and I went back a number of times to have this done.

I went back in again for six weeks of the summer, 1948, when I was fourteen years of age for an op needed before I left school. These were perhaps six of the happiest weeks of my young life.

I was in the hospital this time for an op to try and get more movement into my ankle because I wanted to go into farming when I left school.

This was where I first met Dame Agnes Hunt the owner of the SOH at that time. I met her on Special Ward, this was the ward for all the operations; main ops on a Saturday, minor ops on a Tuesday, where Outpatients is now.

On Friday evening they got me ready for the big day. As I was getting older they had to shave me from the waist down; even the hair on my toes had to be shaved off. Then they painted me with iodine from the waist down, and to top it all I was bandaged up like a mummy — I thought I was on fire!

Dame Agnes came round the ward to comfort all the patients before their gas and she was lovely. Dame Agnes I believe was having an op the same day for an ingrowing toe nail.

I ended up back on the ward Saturday evening with a plaster to the top of my leg.

The reason why these were six happy weeks on the ward was because there were three lads of the same age as me and we became very good friends. Len was from Ludlow with a fractured femur; he had been in for four months. David Jones from Corris had his knee damaged in the drum of a threshing box and Billy Booth from Nantwich had a broken leg. This was a very hot summer, we did some school work but not a lot.

The beds were on wheels and our parents could push us around the hospital grounds. Dad came and would push me down to watch cricket on a Saturday afternoon. Mother used to come during the week.

As you can imagine, when you are fourteen years of age you tend to get a bit naughty from time to time; tormenting the nurses to say the least. This one particular night we wondered

7

who could stay awake the longest. At the end of the ward, over the clock was a pilot light, so one of us hopped out of bed and chucked a pillow slip over the light. Only one night nurse was on duty on the ward and she was as bad as we were; say no more! But two sisters were also on duty and popped into the ward from time to time. Mini and Tich we called them. They were quite savage although only about five feet tall. Well the sisters saw the cover on the light and played hell, saying we would set the hospital on fire. The nurse was told to fetch the night porter. One of the sisters told the porter to push all four of us outside and cover our beds with a waterproof cover. We were there until 7 a.m., but it was quite nice really.

After three weeks I had my plaster removed and twenty-four stitches taken out to be replaced by a short one to the knee. Now when you have a long plaster removed your knee is set and it takes two or three days to get the movement back again. Thinking I was being clever and brave I sat on the edge of my bed and let my leg drop and I let out a howl of pain; something I will never do again.

As we were getting better David, Len and myself had a wheelchair between us and we used to go to Wheatley Ward to play with the little kids and have a go on the big rocking horse.

We had a violent thunderstorm one afternoon. All the wards were open fronted until after the fire in late 1948, so the rain blew into the ward before the nurses had a chance to pull the big curtains (up to 1948 birds and cats came onto the ward, even onto your bed).

I was discharged from hospital ready to go back to school in September 1948. I was discharged without an iron on, the first time since I was four years old, but I did have on a walking plaster. This is a plaster with a heel made onto it to save wear.

This did not last long, when trying to play football with lads I cracked my plaster and it was pinching my leg. Back to the SOH; not a very good welcome; into the plaster room and an Ernie Jellf, I think he was part of the furniture, he had been there for years and looked older than the hospital, cut off my plaster with some stainless steel clippers and seemed a big rough doing the job for some reason. A new plaster was put on and I was sent home on crutches and told they did not want to see me again!

The final operation was performed on Crewe Ward in 1950 but I will tell you more as time goes by.

When I was ten or eleven years old I was able to go to the SOH to outpatients on my own. Firstly my mother would take me to Whitchurch Station to catch the train for Oswestry, and after a while I went on my own. Mother used to give me a ten shilling note and that would take me by train to Oswestry, change for Park Hall Halt to the hospital, back to Oswestry, a meal at the Conway chip shop and back to Whitchurch, all for ten bob.

# Down Memory Lane

*A collection of articles written for a local journal*

My mother was born on 14th October 1897 at Undercliff Street, Bradford, West Yorkshire. Brought up in a very religious family, being a Wesleyan, which she kept up all through her life. Mother met my father-to-be while he was on leave from the army in the 1914-18 War. They became engaged and married in Bradford after the war. They moved to Ash, a small village on the outskirts of Whitchurch after they were married.

Mum and Dad did not have a very good start to married life, having four children, Louise born in 1922, twins Arthur and John born in 1924 and Kathleen born in 1926. Mother moved into a row of houses called Cateralls Lane. A girl in the lane was a carrier of scarlet fever and carried it to Mum's children, and by 1926 three children had died, leaving Mum with just Arthur, one of the twins, who almost died as well .

People who remember Mother can recall how slight a woman she was, very slim and less than five feet tall. Mum and Dad then moved to a house in Whitchurch, moving into Fountain House where the big car park is now on the main Shrewsbury to Chester Road. They then moved to a new council house, moving in as I understand even before the windows were put in the sitting room. I don't suppose that would happen today.

After moving in, three more children were born, Phillip, Margaret and Mum kept the best until last, ME. Arthur is ten years older than me so I always remember Arthur as a young man and must say was always good to me as a child. As you can understand Mother was never the same after losing three children, she was very weepy and could never go to chapel because the hymns upset her. But she led a very good life in her own home.

Mum was very strict, good manners were the order of the day. Bad language was never used by Mum or Dad and I never use it. Alcohol was a crime, also I remember Mum going to Arthur's wedding and Phillip saying Mum and the minister were the only two who never had a drink, not even a toast. I must also say that I never drank until I met June and I don't enjoy drinking but I suppose you have to be sociable from time to time.

As a lad, walking out with Mum, you always had to walk on the outside and keep in step. Mother always liked to be outside in the garden or going shopping. When we were short of food, Mother would go without to make sure her children were fed. A good cook was Mum, who could make a meal very cheaply.

Dad was never at home a lot. He was at work in the day and going to my uncles on the summer nights or working in his allotment. We saw more of Dad on winter nights. Mother always wanted a farm but Dad wanted to stay in Whitchurch, which was quite understandable really as he was born in the area. But in 1951 we did move to Wales.

We lived in Hirnant for thirteen years and Mother loved every minute of it. Mum and Dad moved with me to Brwynen in 1964 and started to farm all over again. I married in 1970 and left Mum, Dad, Phillip and Kath at Brwynen. Dad died in 1974 at the age of eighty-one. Kath married and left Mum and Phillip at Brwynen. Mum died in 1981 aged eighty-four, leaving Phillip at Brwynen until he married Mary.

Mum and Dad lived a good life and she achieved what she had always wanted, a farm. Rest in Peace Mum and Dad.

Dad was born the second oldest son of Arthur Dawson in 1894 in the small rural village of Ash, just outside Whitchurch.

As I remember, Uncle Ted farmed at Old Hall Farm, a dairy farm of eighty-four acres, Uncle Fred farmed at Villa Farm, sixty-five acres, Uncle Joe farmed at Fish Pond, sixty-two acres and Grandfather and Uncle Bert farmed at Meadows Farm, eighty-two acres, all selling milk in churns in those days. All four farms joined each other, making quite a big unit.

Every Sunday afternoon without fail, Dad would visit his brothers and finish the day milking by hand at Grandad's, (mostly shorthorn cows in the 40s). Starting at Uncle Fred's to collect his gun and terrier, old Nell, we would go from farm to farm across the fields with big hedges, a haven for rabbits and pheasants. Nell would flush out the rabbits or the odd bird and Dad would bowl them over. He was a good shot was Dad. A box of twenty-five cartridges was 25/- as I recall and rabbits were fetching 2/- or 2/6 each and the skins 6d (six pence). Dad would milk, and then work his way back to Uncle Fred's, having a few more rabbits on the way home. He would leg the rabbits in pairs and hang them on the handlebars. I would sit on a seat on the crossbar. The journey home was about two and a half miles.

Dad's work was an agricultural engineer for W. H. Smith and a lot of the time in the summer months was spent repairing mowing machines and binders for farmers for miles around and if the job was after working hours the money was extra to his work but sometimes it was a day's ferreting in the winter instead.

1 used to go with Dad after school if he repaired binders,

because he would be picked up by a farmer at the house and I would go for a ride in the car. Dad would repair the binder and try it out. If it was working OK Dad would have a gun off the farmer and shoot the rabbits as the binder got close to the middle of the field. We had a nice supper, and then were taken home.

Sundays in the winter months were always spent catching rabbits until it was time to go to Grandpa's for milking. My brother Arthur would put six gills (female ferrets) in a box for the job, and the liner (a male ferret with a collar on and a ferret line) was put in a sand bag in some straw. The idea was get a rabbit warren, net all the holes you could find with purse nets (a net with a peg to hold it to the ground with a running loop so that when the rabbit ran into the net the purse net would go tight hence purse net). Holes all netted, put the gills in the holes under the nets and wait for the fun.

Rabbits would bolt into the nets and you had to be quick because sometimes two rabbits would come to the same net and you would lose one if you didn't put your foot in the hole in time. The gills would come to the net to look for the rabbit and then go back into the warren to look for another. When all your gills came out of the warren it was time to move to the next one.

But sometimes one would stay down if the rabbit would not bolt, they would tuck up at the end of the hole to stop the ferret getting past him (usually an old buck rabbit), this was where your liner was used. Getting your hob (as they are known) out of the bag, putting your line on his collar and then drop him into a hole. Off he would go and sometimes come back. Then you had to put him into another hole until he found the gill. The gill would come out but the hob would stay with the rabbit. He would either get past the rabbit and bolt him or stay with the rabbit and kill it. Then you would have to dig until you came near to the rabbit. On your line you would have two markers. Two knots on your line would mean two yards from your ferret and one knot would mean one yard. Now when you come to your one knot, that is where the fun started. Dig a little nearer put your arm up the hole, get your ferret out, then put your arm up again and pull out your rabbit, ring its neck and put your ferret in again and you might have one or two more rabbits. I have seen my dad nearly standing on his head pulling rabbits out of deep holes covered in sand but loving his sport.

Two good rabbiting tales before I finish. We went to Hocknell's, Yew Tree Farm, Wrenbury, Nr Nantwich. Ferreting all morning and had one rabbit very deep in a sand warren. Mr Hocknell had sent his farm worker to cut some brambles and blackthorn bushes around a small warren out from the hedge. After dinner we went to ferret this warren. Arthur didn't bother with the gills. Dad just used the hob and he wouldn't go down the hole. Dad took off his trilby and pushed it into the hole to stop him coming out. After a while he did go and he made a strike, it was not very deep and they soon got to the rabbits. Seven there were and what had happened was when the farm workers had cut the brambles it had caused the rabbits to all tuck up at the end of the hole. The first two rabbits pulled out were alive, the next three had been smothered and were pulled out dead and the last two were alive, so we had eight rabbits. Mr Hocknell wanted two so we had six to take home. Mr Hocknell gave Dad a big bottle of Woodpecker cider to have with his tea. Dad gave me a drink and said "Don't tell your mother when you get home." Mother was a big TT and I don't mean tea tea either.

The best laugh I had was stalking rabbits at Polly Ruckas, next to Grandpa's farm. What was following us but an escaped parrot of some sort and every time Dad was about to shoot a rabbit, this parrot would start squawking and disturb the rabbits. This went on for a while until Dad got fed up and shot the parrot and pushed it down a rabbit hole out of sight.

My father was born in the village of Ash, on the outskirts of Whitchurch, he was the second son out of seven boys and was born in 1894.

Four generations of the Dawson family all worked for the same firm of W. H. Smith & Sons, an agricultural engineering firm, the main employer in the town. They made cheese presses, stationary balers, etc. They also had gangs going out putting up hay barns etc. Dad started work as an apprentice fitter, starting work at 2/6 per week (less than 12½p in new money).

Dad served his time in the 1914-18 War in the Royal Engineers. During his war service he met my mother and married her after the war. After the war he worked for nearly forty years for W. H. Smith before moving to Wales in 1951. Dad never really wanted to move but left for mother's sake.

As I say Dad was the second son of Arthur Dawson who was by trade an engineer but had to take up farming after my grandmother's two brothers died. They had left the farm to Walter, Dad's oldest brother who had been brought up by his two uncles. Now Walter was a bit 'Countryfide' and the shock of losing his uncles and being left the farm was too much for him and was found hanging in the cart shed. The farm was then taken over by my grandparents. I don't remember Grandmother but remember Grandad very well, he died in the mid 50s around eighty-four years.

I remember Dad telling me that Grandmother used to peel a white bucketful of potatoes each day to feed seven boys, Mum and Dad and a maid, but at least they grew their own veg. Rabbits and game would be the main meat. Shorthorn cattle were kept and Grandad would make butter to be sold at Whitchurch market each Friday. I don't think they made cheese like the big farms did. The milk was not collected like it is today. If you did sell milk it had to be taken to the dairies by horse-drawn milk float, in twelve gallon churns.

After the First World War (1914-18), where four of the boys served, as they married they rented farms in the village. Joe at Fish Pond, Edward at Village Farm and Fred at Villa Farm. Bert stayed at home with Grandad at the Meadows. Bert was the only boy never married. Uncle Bill, the black sheep of the family was afraid of nothing and nobody. Dad never farmed on his own until moving to Wales and that was not his type of farming anyway.

My first recollection of my great dad was when he used to visit me at Gobowen Hospital in 1937 and he and my eldest brother Arthur would cycle from Whitchurch each Sunday to visit me. Mother would travel by train from time to time as she could afford.

When I grew older Dad would take me with him on a saddle made on the crossbar of his cycle, as I had a straight leg with an iron calliper on it, it would stick out towards the pavement or the hedge and that's how we travelled around for years until I cycled myself. Dad was the sole breadwinner, married women with children did not go out to work like today, they looked after the home and family.

After work in the summer, Dad was a keen gardener and we had a big allotment on the Chester Road where Dad and Arthur grew everything and also sold a lot of veg. From the allotment Dad would take me and I would just potter around until I was able to help a little.

But my favourite times were when Dad would go to repair a mowing machine or a binder. The time he took me to Bradshaw's, Heath Lane Farm, Prees, to put a new connecting rod on a mowing machine which had been cutting a field of flax or now known as linseed. Linseed is very sticky and had gummed up the mower, causing the connecting rod to break. Dad had to unstick the mower with diesel which took some time. The linseed was cut in swathes then carried loose to the thrashing box to be thrashed, a lot of wasted seed as you can tell but now it is all combined. In the next field were carrots as long as your arm and Dad went home with a bag. Mr Bradshaw told Dad he had trouble with rabbits in a field of swedes near the main road and told Dad he could have a day rabbiting instead of paying for the repair to the mower. This was just up Dad's street because that is what he loved, a day's ferreting and shooting. Dad was a great shot, he would not shoot anything unless it was moving, not like me.

We went one Saturday afternoon, a lovely dry day and in among the swedes the rabbits had dug temporary holes just to shelter in, if you understand. In would go the ferret on a line and tug, you could feel the jump and that was it, now dig, it was so shallow, only about four inches below the surface, it was lovely black marl, you didn't need a spade, just your heel of the boot. Dad would pull out the rabbits, we had twenty or more in no time.

He got called out to a binder just out of town, cutting a field of oats and it needed new canvases putting on. These were to carry the cut corn from the bed to the sheaves. Sure enough Dad put on a new set of canvases, tried out the binder and then for the fun. Mr Maddox, Moss Farm, lent Dad a 12 bore and a box of cartridges and as you got towards the end of cutting, out would pop the rabbits. Bang! Bang! A gun at each corner of the field. Mr Maddox's dad was shooting and had an Irish Red Setter which picked up all the dead rabbits. What a great day's sport, nothing like that today.

On a sadder note, Dad went out to a binder, at Jack Oakley's, out on the Malpas Road. I got a bit bored and went after butterflies. We only wore short trousers then and reaching after a butterfly I fell in a ditch full of nettles and started to howl. Dad and Mr Oakley came to see what was the matter. Sure enough Dad got the dock leaves galore, the only cure, and Mr Oakley gave me half a crown (2/6). I seemed to stop crying then.

Dad was a bit naughty really, we went to the allotments one day and he gave me £5. Dad liked a flutter on the horses, but Mother didn't know you see! Well what he had done was put a £1 bet on Russian Hero in the Grand National at 100-1. This was a local horse, trained at Malpas I think and everybody in the town backed it, but what could he do with £100 without mother knowing? He smoked quite heavy too, always Players and always did the pools up until he died.

I never remember Dad swearing or going into a pub, when as a boy he was my hero then. He always liked football and always came with me to support Llanwddyn.

Every year Dad only had one week's holiday from work in the summer and one week between Christmas and the New Year. The whole works closed down for this period.

The only holidays we had away, were a day in Chester, Manchester and Shrewsbury. The day in Chester was on the train (when trains were steam) from Whitchurch Station via Malpas, a line which had closed before we left Whitchurch. Chester Zoo was our favourite; Upton Zoo, it was called then. Mother would always take food because eating out was less to be had than it is today. To finish the day, was shopping in the city and then home on the train.

The day to Manchester was the same, on the train via Crewe. Bell Vue Zoo was going then, not like Chester, more like Blackpool, a pleasure beach as well as the zoo. I never liked things like the big dipper or big wheel, but one year Phillip wanted me to go on what they called the Moon Rocket which went round at an angle. That finished my day, sick don't talk. Another year we went, it was so hot you could hardly breathe. Shopping round the city it went very dark. A thunderstorm on the way. Trams were running around the city in those days and when the storm did come, lightning was hitting the overhead cables on the trams and I was very frightened and glad to get the train home.

Shrewsbury was very nice, most of the day was spent in Percy Thrower's Dingle, feeding the ducks on the Severn and cricket on the grass. Dad always made sure I had my cricket bat and tennis ball. I have never liked Shrewsbury for shopping because of my leg. When I had a calliper to the top of my leg I found it hard to get around the steep streets. I loved the ride on the train to Shrewsbury because it was flatter and you could see a long way.

Perhaps the best line was the old Cambrian Line between Whitchurch and Oswestry. I understand from my dad that the line around Fenn's Bank, Bronington and Whixhall was laid on a bog, built on oak trees laid across the bog to act as a pontoon line and as you crossed this part of the journey the train swayed from side to side. Safe enough I suppose because the old locos didn't go very fast. The two engines that did this run were in the Manor class. One was called Hinton Manor and the other Kingston Manor. Two lovely old steam engines and were always dark green as all Cambrian engines were. This was a single line so you only met another train when you passed through a station. We used this line a lot when Mum or Dad would take me to Gobowen Hospital. There was a line running from Oswestry to Gobowen in those days and I think the station for the hospital was called Park Hall Halt.

I was a very keen train spotter as a boy and I have been around the engine sheds at Crewe where most of the LMS engines were maintained and what massive locos they were when you are at ground level looking up at them. Dad knew how keen I was on train spotting and one Friday he was being taken to the United Dairy's cheese factory adjoining Bakewell Station in Derbyshire. Now between Bakewell and Buxton stations was the steepest gradient in the British Isles taking two engines to pull trains up this line. Dad wanted to show me the line while we were there. What a lovely run it was even though I was stuck in the back of this bumpy old van.

Into Derbyshire, I remember we had to stop from time to time for blasting in the limestone quarries. A man would be standing on the road with a red flag. After the bang he would wave a green flag and then we could move. We got to Bakewell around 1 p.m., had dinner and then Dad put new wooden presses into the machines, then he took me to look up the line. No wonder you could hear the wheels squeaking as the engines went past, the gradient was one in four which is steep for a rail track.

Not to be so lucky on the way home, a broken half shaft was to be sustained on the way. We had to leave the van driver and make our way to the nearest station. I don't know what station it was but we had to change at Crewe to get home to Whitchurch around 12 p.m. Dad was not very pleased because he had to pay my rail fare home.

Dad loved keeping breeding rabbits and always kept around 100 of different breeds. He always kept them in a square facing inwards with a gate at one corner. He kept four males for breeding and they did stink. One was nasty and would bite if you put your finger near the wire. Dad sold the meat from the rabbits, also the skins which would fetch 6d to 1/- each. Phillip and Margaret used to show the rabbits in the town from time to time. I used to go with Mother to collect dandelions from around the rail track. Ferrets were also kept and dead rabbits were fed to them once a week.

We also kept around twenty Brown Leghorn Light Sussex hens in batteries to keep us in eggs and a few to sell. I used to have a card in front of each hen to record her laying. I also collected the eggs after coming home from school. If any of the hens didn't lay for two days and miss a day she had to go. Most of the hens would lay three days and miss a day. Some would lay four days. Hybrid hens today will lay six eggs per week.

This was around the time when Mother was getting uneasy and wanted to start a new life in the country as we had by now all left school and there was no future in a council house.

As a boy in Whitchurch when I was around ten or eleven years old, trains were trains, lovely steam trains, hundreds of them.

Where we lived at 24 Talbot Street you could hear the trains passing through Whitchurch Station, very busy in the 30-40s. Whitchurch was on the main line from Crewe to Shrewsbury, with two branch lines one to Malpas, the other the Cambrian line to Oswestry.

Now at the top of our street, a big suspension bridge spanned the width of the railway lines, around seventy-five yards; a footpath really over to Ash village, but this is where people did train spotting. You could buy train spotting books from W. H. Smith's in the town, one LMS (London Midland and Scottish) and the other GWR (Great Western Railway). The other two zones were, LNER (London North Eastern Railway) and SR (Southern Railway), they never passed through Whitchurch Station.

My great-grandfather fell under a truck, crossing to work, early twentieth century, amputating his leg, but he did work again after a long period.

My first interest was the trains shunting trucks in the siding, bringing the goods and coal to the town. What the trains would do was, the guard would uncouple the trucks to be shunted into the sidings, the train would reverse fast, slam on his brakes and the trucks that had been uncoupled would be left to run into buffers or other trucks with the guard waiting to either couple the trucks up or put on the truck brakes.

Where my father worked had a line running through the works

for unloading scrap iron etc. and loading machines (stationary bailers and cheese presses) made by W. H. Smith & Sons.

From Oswestry came the GWR trains with Hinton Manor bringing in the passenger trains and the little tanker engines, the goods trains. All engines had names or numbers, so they go into your little book just like registrations on cars. AW, UJ, UX and UY are Shropshire; number EP, for Montgomeryshire. It was the same with trains, see a train number, look in your book and you could tell where it came from.

In the holidays or any Mondays around 11 a.m., we were very lucky in Whitchurch because engines came from the Crewe work shops to be tested on the run from Crewe via Nantwich Station because of the incline between the two stations. It was uphill all the way, a test for the engine. We were allowed to go and watch them put on the big turntable to be turned around for the journey home. This was done by each engine, uncoupled and run onto a line over a big round pit. Two men, one either end of the engine with a shaft fitted to the turntable, could turn a engine by hand quite easily. The engineers would go round each engine to feel if the bearings had got too hot, while other men would polish up the engines. Three engines would then couple up and puff back to Crewe, the busiest engine works in the country at that time.

This is why I say Whitchurch Station was good for train spotters because we saw engines that had been repaired, that were quite rare. I have been right by the Royal Scot, now based at Llangollen I believe, the Queen Mary and the streamlined Coronation, massive engines all steam and power.

On Fridays it was Whitchurch cattle market day (sadly gone now), and buyers from long distances would have the cattle they had bought, driven by drovers to the station siding, loaded into cattle trucks made to carry stock on the railway.

During the war a Red Cross train passing through the station was shot at by a German fighter plane which was later shot down.

A game we used to play was, as an express train went under the bridge, run through the smoke and steam (because the floor of the bridge was made with sleepers with a gap of one to two inches between each sleeper) so the smoke would go up your legs (when I went to school you wore short trousers until you nearly left school) and the smoke and steam stung your legs.

We used the trains a lot to travel. The GWR to Oswestry to go to the hospital, the line to Crewe led to Manchester for shopping, the line to Malpas led to Chester for a day out, and the same for Shrewsbury, so you see Whitchurch was a very busy line.

I started my school days in the Shropshire Orthopaedic Hospital, but when I started school at home Phillip used to take me to school on a three-wheeler bicycle. As I had an iron to the top of my leg my leg had to be tied to the handlebars. As I got older I was able to walk with a straight leg until I was eleven years old then I had an iron just to the knee until I left school.

Now I was unable to play and rough it with other children because of my leg so I became a bit of a nature boy, in more ways than one!

Not too far away, you were out in the country and across two fields there was a lovely brook, Stag's Brook (I say a lovely brook — I took our Ian there when he was ten or eleven and the lovely brook was very badly polluted with farm effluent and not a lot of pond life left in the brook).

My dad had four glass tanks which I think had been batteries at one time, eighteen inches by twelve inches and eighteen inches deep. These were to be my aquariums for a number of years. Arthur and Phillip used to go to Stag's Brook and catch all sorts of pond life and put them in the tanks for me to watch and enjoy, either through the window or out on the back yard.

As I got older and was able to go and catch things for myself. Things got a little more interesting because I used each tank for different things. In one tank I would have tadpoles, great crested newts, which were plentiful in those days but are now quite rare, the male being very beautiful with a crest all the way down its back and tail and a lovely russet tummy. The tadpoles I kept for feeding other creatures.

In another tank I kept sticklebacks, the male being very colourful with a red breast. In another tank were kept dragonfly larva, great diving beetle larva, water scorpions, caddis larva, etc. And in the last tank were kept water snails for all tanks, to keep them clean, swan mussels, whirligig beetles, water boatmen, leeches and other bugs. The dragonfly and diving beetle larva were fed mainly on sticklebacks and tadpoles, both had fang-like jaws which shot out when food came near them.

When the dragonfly larva were ready to change to an adult they would climb up a cane put in the tank for this purpose, and what a change!! If anyone has seen this happen will know what I mean. They climb up the cane, settle and literally change from larva to a beautiful dragonfly. This takes at least three-quarters to one hour. It has to be very warm and sunny so as to dry their wings which vibrate for quite a while and then off they go into the open air.

The male stickleback, who you can always tell by his red breast, always looks after the young and woe betide any intruder because he is very vicious. I have watched them in the tanks and have seen them kill tadpoles and even eat their own young in temper. He is a very proud father.

As I got older I used to paddle in the brook with my net and by now used to know where to catch what I wanted. Other kids would come with me but would not take their shoes off. They would say things like "The water scorpions will sting and the leeches will suck your blood." Always when you climbed out of the brook, four or five leeches would be stuck to your legs and took quite a bit of pulling off, leaving blood on your legs.

Stag's Brook ran out of Blake Mere and through the town, but where I went fishing was near to the mere where it ran under the railway. By the mere itself was a grid to stop course fish coming down the brook, but it needed some repair and fish could get through. By the railway itself was a mill pond which was quite deep and you could sit on the side of the brook on a sunny day and watch thousands of young sticklebacks (we called them tiddlers) swimming in shoals, up and down the pool.

One day, on the side of the pool in the sedges, I saw what I thought was a stick. I went to pick it out of the water, but what it was, was a massive pike. When I got hold of it, it gave a mighty splash and shot off back towards the mere. With the fright I fell in the pool with all my clothes on. I went home, got a good hiding for getting all my clothes wet. You canner win, can yer?

I will now tell you about my experiences of ornithology as a schoolboy in Whitchurch. I must admit as a lad I did have a collection of birds' eggs, but it was not against the law in those days. Most boys and some girls did have a collection of eggs at sometime or another and exchanged them like fag cards, marbles, matchboxes, etc., but I collected my own and kept them in a properly-made box with records under each egg.

I had a collection of around seventy eggs when we left Whitchurch and I left them with my mate from next door and he went on to be a game warden. Even though eggs were collected, there were more birds about then than there are today, mainly because game keepers etc. were allowed to shoot vermin; hawks, foxes, stoats, weasels, crows, magpies, jays, etc. Now we have badgers, squirrels, mink, pesticides and insecticides, but I still maintain birds need solitude, which they don't get today. When I was a boy, my dad would show me bitten and corncrake, which are nearly extinct today, mainly from mowing early and spoiling their habitat.

Our family were all keen gardeners and when we were young we had a very large allotment just outside the town on the Tarperely Road, and I tell you we could grow anything there the soil was so good. I was unable to help a lot because of my leg, so I used to sprot around looking for birds' nests at the bottom of the garden in a big hawthorn hedge. One particular day I found a hedge sparrow's nest with just one egg in it, so I thought I would record this nest. Sure enough by the end of the week she had laid four eggs. The following week I looked at the nest again and there were still four eggs but one was bigger and a different colour, so I called my dad to come and look and he said a cuckoo had taken one egg and laid her own egg instead.

Now sure enough I went every night after school to observe the nest and the three hedge sparrow's eggs hatched first and then the cuckoo two days later, not a lot bigger than the hedge sparrow chicks.

The next day I went down the garden, one hedge sparrow chick left in the nest, the other two were in the hedge bottom, one dead the other alive. I put the live one back into the nest to see what would happen. The young cuckoo then started to lift the hedge sparrow chicks out of the nest with like a hole in the back, pushing and heaving until it went over the side of the nest. I then left as the two parent birds wanted to feed the chicks.

Dad told me to leave the nest alone as this is nature with cuckoos and some smaller birds. I went back a week later and sure enough one big, fat cuckoo was left in the nest. Now the cuckoo grew bigger and bigger and I used to pick it out of the nest and stroke its back until it became quite tame. It was in the nest for about two weeks and then it was gone. I used to wonder how many children had recorded a cuckoo like that!

We had a bird table at home and I used to write down how many different birds came to the table. The tit and finch families were most common. We never had grey squirrels like we have today, another pest that will take eggs and chicks out of the nests. I remember my dad finding a sparrow hawk sitting in an old crow's nest and each egg was a slightly different colour. I wonder whether this is uncommon RSPB?

On a Sunday Dad would take me on the crossbar on his bicycle to Grandad's farm to help Uncle Bert milk his cows, by hand those days. While they were milking I would wander off round the fields. Grandad had big high hawthorn bushes growing out into his fields, a haven for wildlife. I came across a pair of long-eared owls sitting close together in a bush, quite tame really, turning their heads nearly round watching me. One was a head bigger than the other. Dad told me later that all female owls are bigger than the male. Is this true RSPB?

One afternoon on a trip to Brown Moss with Mum and Dad (a beauty spot just out of town, a peat bog area, a haven for pond life as the water is shallow and peaty, dragonfly and damsel fly in abundance). I stumbled on a skylark's nest. This is a lovely bird which lay an egg scribbled all over, as if by a ballpoint pen. A lovely place for a picnic but watch the ants in your pants.

When we moved to Wales in 1951, different birds were to be seen, such as buzzards, flycatchers, redstarts, stonechats, whinchats, dipper and many more. I once recorded a great grey backed strike at Llechwedd-Du, but around Whitchurch there were birds like house sparrows and starlings which we were glad to be rid of really. Yellowhammers, greenfinch, long tailed tits, cuckoos, sand martins and song thrushes were very common.

I will now tell you a good story. Emlyn Jones was headmaster and warden at the school and I was working with Jack at the old pickler. One Saturday morning I was on the lakeside collecting a load of firewood for Jack and myself and we were home to Churchstoke in the afternoon. Seeing six goosanders on the lake near the old pickler on the way home, I called at the school house and told Emlyn about them. (A big mistake really because I nearly missed the match.) Emlyn got out his telescope and binoculars and asked me to go with him to where I had seen them. He would have it they would have been goldeneyes not goosanders. Arriving at the place where I had seen them, they had gone. Out came Emlyn's binoculars and he could see they had drifted over towards the tower. Round the top end he had to go to get to the tower, stopping every time he spotted a bird on the lake. By the time we got to the tower the goosanders were drifting back towards the pickler and they were goosanders, and that's when they were first recorded on the lake; winter 1961, I nearly missed the game. Eddie Shop was stand-in ref and I think this was when Llanwddyn had the record score of beating Churchstoke 11-? (correct me if I'm wrong).

As I have written before, I have always been interested in nature and the countryside. As a boy I always went rough shooting with Dad and during the war and after we never went short of food. We had rabbits, snipe, mallard and woodcock. You name it, Dad shot it. Also we had eggs of moorhen, wild duck and pheasant, plus the peewit which Mother would use for baking. This was a common thing for country people to live on, that is why they were put on this earth.

You never took all of the eggs of course, one or two from each nest. Now if you found a nest with quite a number of eggs you let it alone because they would be in incubation and not fit to eat, and if you found a lapwing's nest with four eggs with points of the eggs together, they were sitting, two or three, take one, she would lay another.

Now, the reason for the decline — because there is a decline — not only in the peewits, but sky larks, curlews and most ground nesting birds and what about the decline in the hedgehog. The decline is due to the 80% increase in the badger population and the great increase in the bird of prey. Don't keep blaming the farmers, because they are the ones who would like to keep the balance right.

I have been in farming in one form or another for over fifty years and walking around with my eyes open and notice what goes on around me. In 1964-65-66 we went into a small farm scheme at Brwynen Pen-y-Geuffordd and Brynheddyn which entailed ploughing all the ground that could be ploughed and reseeding. This was a three-year plan and was run by Clive Scott.

Now Phillip ploughed thirty acres of Brwynen mountain in three ten-acre plots, rape the first year, reseeded the next. The peewits and curlews nested for a number of years in abundance, then came the increase in the badger and now the hawk family and you never see a peewit.

We travel to Market Drayton quite often and see plenty of peewit in that area but little badger population as I understand.

Go on Brwynen fields or mountain and you would think I kept pigs but this is not so, it is due to the badger rooting for pig nuts or grubs. This has never been seen until latter years. Look at the number killed on the roads and you can tell what the population must be. The badger will eat anything and the ground nesting bird has not got a chance. They will take eggs and fledglings in their path. Why do we not see hedgehogs? Because the badger loves them dead or alive. If hawks will take pigeons in flight, what chance has the peewit!

What I am trying to say in my story is this. When I was a boy there were plenty of birds due mainly to good gamekeepers who were not told "Don't shoot this and don't shoot that" and were controlled in a right and proper manner.

If small birds are to survive we have to have a balance.

I suppose my first experience of football was when, as you might say, I was thrown in at the deep end.

My cousin Victor asked me, when I was about eleven years of age, if I would like to go to the first football match after the war (in 1946), and watch Stoke City play Preston North End at the Victoria Ground, Stoke. Victor, Dad and myself, went in Victor's old Rover car. I suppose about twenty-five miles from Whitchurch. I think the gate was 80,000 plus because it was a big attraction. Stoke had four internationals in the team, Stanley Matthews, Billy Steel, Frank Mountford and Neil Franklin, and Preston had Tom Finney.

Not a lot of noise at the match like there is today and no hugging and kissing. When you scored a goal no singing just a hum of people talking. I didn't understand the rules of the game, like offsides etc., but you could charge the keeper into the back of the net and score a goal that way. If it was wet, the ball was like lead and it took a good goalkeeper to reach the halfway line with a goal kick, and if you headed the ball wrongly you were knocked out for a while.

I think Preston won 1-0 but I am not sure. Now at half-time you never had a drink unless you took one with you and there were no fire escapes, just row after row of people. I know we were in the stand, but in the second half what did Brian want to do? You have a guess, he wanted to go to the toilet. "Dad," sez I, "I want to go to the toilet."

"You will have to wait until after the match" sez Dad.

"I can't wait" sez I. So I wet my pants. But they were dry by the time I arrived home because Dad gave me a newspaper to sit on.

Now that was a big game to kick off with, crowds were big at matches in the 40s and 50s. No TV and no safety regulations either. I then started to watch the local team play. Whitchurch Alport, just up the road from where we lived; Black Park Road at Yocking's Park. Before the war as I understand from my dad, the Whitchurch team was captained by a Colie Maddox who was killed during the war. He was the oldest son of the Alport Dairy Farm and in his memory, after the war they named the Whitchurch team after him.

They play in the Mid-Cheshire League now, but when I used to watch them, they played in the old Shropshire League Division 1, playing teams like Wem, Whixhall, Prees, Hadnall, Ruyton 11 Towns and Baschurch, to name a few.

Now Whitchurch Reserves play in that league. I just went to home matches as the reserves had mostly local players, but the 1st team were mostly from Crewe and Nantwich, (like Llanwddyn at one time I suppose had players from Llanfyllin etc.).

I supported Whitchurch from 1946 until moving to Wales in 1951 and the only time I missed a match was when I went with Harry to Crewe. Even though I had a bad leg I had plenty of mates and one of my mate's brothers played for the reserves. Eric Hinton was his name and he played right half. It was different then watching a match. Each player marked a man so closely that they nearly got inside the other player's shorts; the players went round the pitch in pairs. This was why Stanley Matthews was so good. He shielded the ball so well and always tried to get his back to his opponent and had to be tackled from behind, hence a free kick. Who took the free kick but Stanley and it was nearly always from the right wing. He never strayed far.

The best I remember Whitchurch doing was when they were in the Shropshire League, when they got to the final of the Ethelstone Cup. The cup I understand in value is worth more in silver than any other football trophy.

Whitchurch Alport v Wem Town, and I remember it was a local man who scored the winning goal for Whitchurch, a player called Bobby Jones, a little bald chap about five feet two inches, who ended up in the back of the net, goalkeeper, ball and all from a corner. Whitchurch is quite a big town but very poorly supported, then I suppose we were stuck between Manchester, Stoke and Shrewsbury, but you cannot beat local football.

Whitchurch went into the Mid-Cheshire League in 1948 and played very strong teams, semi-pros mostly. When I was secretary of Llanwddyn I tried to arrange a friendly with the reserves. I did write to Bernard Painter the Whitchurch Secretary but he could not fit Llanwddyn in at the time. The last game I saw Whitchurch play was at Wrexham in 1957 or 1958. Chirk AAA v Whitchurch Alport in the final of the Welsh Amateur Cup, played at the Racecourse. Henry came with me on the old Royal Enfield 350cc and I know Whitchurch still had two old players in the team, Vic Platt in goal and a player called Wildblood. Chirk won 1-0 but it was a good game just the same.

I picked up football again in Llanwddyn in 1956, "the good old days!"

As a boy in Whitchurch, we lived in a council house with quite a large garden, which had two feet of loam over red sand and you could dig the garden all the year round.

During the war Dad and Arthur, my oldest brother, dug an air-raid shelter at the bottom of the garden. While digging through the red sand they filled the sandbags to make the shelter walls, reinforcing the roof with railway sleepers. I cannot remember using the shelter for air raids but we did play hide-and-seek in it and Dad used to store potatoes, carrots, etc. during the winter.

Arthur made me a cold frame but I used it for breeding butterflies and moths from caterpillars. During the war we kept a lot of rabbits for meat and pelts. Phillip also used to show rabbits in the town. Dad's job was breeding the rabbits but Mother, Margaret and myself had to collect food for them during the summer. This was how I found out about caterpillars and butterflies.

Caterpillars (Peacock and small Tortoiseshell) bred on stinging nettles so this was how I started putting nettles and caterpillars into the cold frame and adding other breeds of caterpillars and the right feed when I found them. Garden canes were put into the frame for the caterpillars to change into pupa by hanging from the canes. Some rolled up inside a leaf, others just laid on the dry soil. A meal sack was laid over the cold frame to save it getting hot on sunny days.

What a lovely sight to watch the butterflies hatch from pupa. Each day in late summer the cold flame lid was lifted to allow the butterflies to be liberated. Also all the hawk moth family were kept, these were bigger and fatter than butterfly caterpillars and did not hatch until the spring.

Arthur bought for me my first butterfly display box. Dad showed me how to display the butterflies in the box by pinning the butterfly and pinning strips of paper across its wings to hold them in the right place. After I got used to displaying them myself I had more boxes made by Arthur with balsa wood bottoms to make it easy for pinning. What I used to like was a display of a male upper-side and a male under-side, and a female upper-side and a female under-side of each species I could catch, making a complete set if you like.

The earliest butterflies you see are the orange tips; the male with the orange tips and the female without, very much like the small white species. In Whitchurch we used to have the Brimstone very early. This is a lovely sulphur yellow butterfly with unusual shaped wings.

I think butterflies are getting fewer because of the change in farming. When I was a boy, corn was set to grow naturally (no spraying for weeds like today), and the so-called weeds were what the butterflies and caterpillars loved, hence the decline in the butterfly.

I think it was the summer of 1948, I know I had been in hospital until late July and it was very hot weather, and I was out with my net and gas mask box which I collected my butterflies in. On this particular day I saw a yellow butterfly which I had never seen before. I caught it on a thistle flower and put it in my box and took it home and pinned it in my display case. It turned out to be a rare Clouded Yellow and it was a male. I did catch quite a number more that summer and did have a set and two spare, male and female.

Now it so happened that we had a daily paper in those days called *The Daily Chronicle* and in a small column at the bottom of the front page was a heading "Clouded Yellow Seen", and it had been seen for the first time in fifty years down the south of England. So I wrote to the editor of the paper for his address and he wrote to me and told me all about the Clouded Yellow. I sent him my two spare butterflies in Swan Vestas matchboxes and he again wrote back to thank me for them. I did keep the letter, written in green ink and he was eighty-four years old.

The same summer I caught another rare butterfly known as the Grayling. This butterfly, alighted very high in bushes and very fast in flight, but I did manage to catch a pair with a very long net.

My favourite butterflies are the Fritillary family, the Comma and the Red Admiral butterflies, so different in size and colour.

Where we lived in Whitchurch, we lived on the Cheshire end of
the town with very rich grass land. Passing the Whitchurch Alport
football ground, and over the old railway bridge over the
Whitchurch to Chester line, Yocking Farm was the first farm
out of the town. The main grazing ground was over the railway
again but this time it was the Crewe to Whitchurch line and the
cows had to pass over this bridge night and morning to be milked.
But they got used to the trains even when the Manchester to
Shrewsbury express passed under them with all the steam blowing
around. Over the bridge was one big field which was never
ploughed, called the forty acre. The other fields were grazed
after hay, corn or root crops had been harvested.

I remember Arthur coming home from work one day and
telling Mother he had had a terrible day. Someone had left a gate
open on to a field of red clover and 'blown' a number of cows;
some had died, some the vet saved. What happens is this. You
get your aftermath, as it is called, after you have had your hay
crop. Firstly you let the cows graze the clover for about an hour
each morning and then fetch them off. If you leave them longer
they gorge themselves, which causes a gas in the cow's body which
simply blows them up. In those days not many telephones had
been installed on farms, so by the time one of the farm workers
had got on his bike and rode to the vets it was too late, the cows
were dead or dying by the time he arrived. I have never seen a
good field of red clover since we left Whitchurch. The clover
flowers were a haven for bees and butterflies and the scent was in
the air for miles, such a lot of clover was grown at that time.

Like all towns and villages we had a 'gang'; Phillip, Margaret and myself, Raymond, Jean and Brian Griffiths next door and David Parry up the street, that was our gang. I always seemed to get away when we were in trouble, not telling the others when someone was coming. Twice I saw Cuthbert, one of Jim's younger brothers coming after us and I sneaked off without telling the gang, not like me to do such a thing really!!

Now Cuthbert was a savage young man, still in college studying to be a doctor and he always seemed to carry a kicking strap used for tying cows' legs to stop them kicking when milking.

We were playing hide-and-seek in a field of wheat stooks which were quite big because they were made of twelve sheaves of corn and you could hide in them. Now I could see Cuthbert coming a long way off and I think I scarpered for home that time. All the rest of the gang got a tanning with the kicking strap and then had to tidy up the stooks before letting them go. Phillip and Margaret came home with sore bums and told me off but Mum came to the rescue and told them off for playing in Jim's corn field. Ha! Ha! I had the last laugh.

The second time he caught them we were making a hide between two stacks of hay; round stacks they were, like the crofters make in Ireland, starting small in the bottom and tapering outwards to run the rain off. Now this time I saw Cuthbert coming but he was coming from towards home, so I had to run away from home, not very easy with an iron to the top of my leg, but it's surprising how fast you can go when someone's after you with a kicking strap. This time I climbed an old oak tree with low branches and went right to the top of the tree in amongst the leaves. After Cuthbert had finished tanning the others he came after me and passed right under the tree where I was hiding and also passed back after he could not find me. I had to stay there, it seemed like hours before I came down, because I knew Cuthbert would be helping to milk by then so I was safe. Phillip only laughed and said "Serves you right."

Yocking Farm was set back off the road, about fifty yards, but you could never pass unless the cattle dog by the name of Gip came barking down the drive. I don't think she was nasty but I always thought she was, until one afternoon I was at the farm and she came barking after me and I went up a ladder into the hay loft, and you know what — she came up the ladder after me and I nearly wet myself because I was trapped and I thought she was going to bite me, but by chance she only wanted to play.

On the farm they had a pair of Chinese geese, and each year they had a good hatch of young which were killed at Christmas time. One year they flew off, all thirteen of them and landed on Blake Mere about two miles away. Only the old pair returned. The young ones never did return alive because Cuthbert came home for Christmas holidays and he borrowed a boat from the Mere keeper and went out onto the Mere and shot them. The old pair were nasty. When they had young they were worse than Gip.

Jim had two shorthorn bulls, one tied with the cows the other in a loose box. By mistake both bulls were let out together and a fight was started and they had to be parted with pitchforks. Quiet bulls really but not when together. Jim took me to a quiet old cow and showed me how to milk. I had a go with just one hand and did squirt a little milk out of one teat.

Yocking Farm had a ghost and the old saying: *Be it early or be it late, I'll wait for thee by Yocking Gate.*

The last thing I remember helping Jim to do was to knock a field of wheat down for carrying. Knocking down the stocks and to open out the butt ends of the sheaves for the sun and the wind to get into them, facing into the wind. You see the wheat had been under-sown with grass and clover seed so there was a lot of green in the sheaves. The field would then be harvested mid-afternoon and evening. During that time it was called double summertime when it was light until 11 p.m.

Jim Luton farmed in Whitchurch. I recall what my dad told me about the early days of the Luton family. In the early 1920s Yocking's Farm, Talbot Street, Whitchurch was farmed by a family of Jones', but after the old man died it came up for sale. A good farm of around 250 acres on the outskirts of the town. Dad told me how the Luton family moved from Ireland to take over the Yocking's farm A family of Mum and Dad and seven children. We lived in Talbot Street ourselves in later years but Dad says how they came to Whitchurch Station with all their belongings on the train moving to the farm with donkey and cart, then to collect stock, etc., they had brought from Ireland later. This was well before my time but I do remember Jim's mother and father, both short and stocky people and they both lived to a very big age.

The older people in the village will perhaps remember Dr Abraham Luton being one of the last surgeons at Oswestry Cottage Hospital in the 1970s. Well he was one of the Luton's oldest sons; Jim was perhaps older. Abraham, Cuthbert and Beth all went on to be doctors. Jim took over the farm and Aggie looked after Mum and Dad.

My first recollection of the Luton family was my oldest brother Arthur working there as a young man in 1940s. Joe Ashley was wagoner and Charlie Mooge was stockman along with Jim and Arthur. By now they were milking eighty dairy Shorthorn cattle along with two Roan Shorthorn bulls, both running out with the cows, one at night and the other during the day.

Joe Ashley did all the horse work with, by now, four black

Shire horses, no tractor until after the war. Jim was a good man, very fond of children and never stopped children going into his cow sheds to look at his cows. I went quite a lot at milking time, four men and sometimes Aggie milking by hand, a sound you never hear today, slurp, slurp, slurp as the milk went in the bucket.

All the harvest was done by hand, cocks of hay and stooks of corn, all carried in by horse and cart. Old man Luton and Joe Ashley sowing corn and grass seed by hand. Mr Luton used to sow with both hands with a much wider broadcast. Joe sowed out of a bath sower, Mr Luton sowed out of a sack converted for the job. When corn was sown it was also sown with red clover and grass ready for hay the following year.

Jim also grew a lot of potatoes and sold them around the town. He grew two Irish varieties, Kerrs Pink and Great Scott, not potatoes liked today because of the deep eyes, not very good for chip making. Dad grew Great Scott but never so good as Jim.

I remember Jim buying his first tractor, it came by rail and I saw it in a rail truck in the railway siding at Whitchurch Station. An old Ford Standard with iron front wheels and spade lugs at the back. This was just after the war and he had this tractor for years. I think he still had it when we left Whitchurch in 1951.

As years passed by Dad did all the machinery repair work for Jim in his work time and his own. In the summer holidays we worked for Jim picking potatoes, pulling swedes and mangolds. This was a job with extra holidays after the war, right up to October when labour was short. Phillip was crafty, he always got the job on the lead horse on the potatoes lifter. This was a very old machine which the Luton family had bought from Ireland. It was very heavy and two Shires and a light horse were used to pull the machine. Phillip rode on the lead horse's back. The beauty of the Kerrs Pink and Great Scott was that they were all big spuds and soon filled your bucket then you had to empty the bucket into 1cwt sacks, this gave you a chance to rest your back.

The soil around Whitchurch was very sandy and very little stones, but some of the pickers found a big stone and put it in the path of the digger and two tines were broken off and needed a blacksmith welding, so that was the end of spud picking for the day. Mangold and swede pulling came next but this job was too hard for me because I was not very old and had to go back to school.

The corn fields were cut with a binder pulled by the two Shires, a lovely sight to see on a good field of wheat. Dad would be there with his 12 bore, popping off the rabbits as they ran from the cutting. Sometimes he would shoot a fox. The sheaves were put into stooks as they were called, but were not sixes like they did in Shropshire, but an Irish way, in twelves, reversing the top six and tying the tops with a twist of straw. In the autumn or winter the thrashing box and baler pulled by a steam engine would be seen passing our house ready for thrashing the next day after being set up by the side of the bays of corn for thrashing.

Jim always liked to thrash on Saturdays because he had cheap labour from the schoolboys. I always had the job on the baler, threading the wires through between each bale. Men had to stack and handle the bales because they were very heavy. Cider and tea were had at intervals but no bun-fight was had at the end of the day, not like in Wales when you always had a lovely dinner after thrashing.

After we left Whitchurch Jim retired and went to live in Oswestry and married late in life, and he and his wife started to collect antiques and got quite a good business going.

The only time I really got to know Abraham Luton was when he performed a gall bladder operation on me in 1976. We got quite friendly and talked about our cattle and farming, and when I was getting better he said to the nurses, "Get Brian ready for home so he can get back to his cows."

Sad, Tim and Abraham have passed on but they have left me with very happy memories.

I have been keeping an every day diary now since 1947 but unfortunately the early ones have gone missing, plus when moving to Wales in 1951 and to Brwynen, they have been misplaced but I thought a few dates from my diaries might be of interest.

*(This is the first entry I can find. I was recovering from an operation I had in 1950 at sixteen years of age and this is how I used to write. I used to help Mother a lot while off work. I had started my first farming job after going to farming college but had to finish because of my ankle.)*

1.1.51   Went to wish Miss Evans, Mrs Beddows and Mrs Tipton a Happy New Year. Tidied the bottom cupboard out. Did more of my rug. Had dinner. Dad came home from work and went to bed with a bad cold. Killed and plucked the last bantam. Fed the ferrets, did more rug. Had tea, did more rug. Went to the pictures with Phillip and Brian. Had supper, did more rug. Went to bed.

25.1.51   Sold 2 ferrets 12/6.

26.1.51   Had plaster cast off my leg. Dr advised another plaster. Went home in ambulance. Uncle Herbert died 87.

27.1.51   Wireless football match: Newport Co 0 -1 Norwich City.

30.1.51   Bought 2 ferrets off John Cotton. 10/- each.

3.2.51   Whitchurch Alp 6 - Northwich Res 2.

7.2.51   Sold 2 rugs 25/- each and got an order for 6' x 4'.

9.2.51   Broke plaster. To SOH for new one. Sent home on crutches.

Friday 16 Feb 1951 Wrestling in Town Hall *(this was every fortnight)*

| | |
|---|---|
| **HASSAN ALI BEY**<br>Heavyweight Champion<br>of Egypt – 16 st.<br>ALI BEY won by 2 falls to 1 | **DEPUTY**<br>Heavyweight Champion<br>of Ireland – 16 st. |
| **DOMINIC PYE**<br>Clean, Clever and Scientific<br>– 14 st.<br>Draw | **BLACK PANTHER**<br>The Coloured Gent of the Ring<br>– 14 st. |
| **RICK ST JUST**<br>The Norwegian Flash<br>St Just won | **JACK MACKENDRICK**<br>Scotland's Pride and Joy |
| **RICK ST JUST**<br>Deputized for Bert Royal<br>Hall won by 2 falls to 1 | **JOHN HALL**<br>Fast coming up the ladder |

21.2.51   Bought iron bedstead 2/6 (just because I nodded my head to my mate). Never sold my rug.

23.2.51   Had plaster removed then went to clinical conference in front of all the doctors. Went home without plaster.

24.2.51   Went with Mum and Dad to see a smallholding in Montgomeryshire, 47 miles away. Arrived 3.35 pm, had a good look around. Home 7.15.

2.3.51   Went to the wrestling.

10.3.51   Went to stay Pen-y-Geuffordd for a week to see if I would like it. Mr and Mrs Atkinson who we bought Pen-y-Geuffordd from met me at Pen-y-bont-fawr station. Caught two rabbits in snares.

*We bought Pen-y-Geuffordd for £1,760 with all the stock and tools, two sows with litters of pigs and the poultry, around fifty birds. But no electricity or water. Water had to be carried 100 yards up hill.*

11.3.51   Mr Atkinson worked for the Liverpool Corporation with Dai Owen from Brwynen, and we went there for supper on this date. Very wild and windy.

12.3.51   Went down to Hirnant village to meet egg van from Llanrhaeadr with a couple of rabbits I had snared. 2/6 each.

13.3.51   Tidied out store shed and saw three rats.

14.3.51   Mr and Mrs Atkinson went to Liverpool so I looked after the holding.

*Mr and Mrs Atkinson did move back to Liverpool, to West Kirby. They were both very keen on bowls and that was the main reason to move back to Liverpool. We moved to Wales with two lorry loads of furniture on the first day of spring 1951 and I remember snow in the hollows around Brwynen and Bwlsych.*

10.1.57   Went to see Mr Howard about a job with Liverpool Corporation.

11.1.57   Thrashing at Cefn.

21.1.57   Started to work for LCWW. Sold sow and litter £45.

8.2.57   Went to the pictures in the hall. "Springfield Rifle".

14.2.57   "Doctor in the house".

20.2.57   Sorted rails and loaded rails with Tom Watkins *(this job went on until the summer of 57).*

7.3.57   Had first lamb.

15.3.57   Pictures: "War Arrow".

18.3.57   Phillip started to work with horse at the Dairy.

22.3.57   Pictures: "The Quiet Man".

29.3.57   Pictures: "Inspector Calls".

5.4.57   Pictures: "Many Rivers To Cross".

7.4.57   Spring scramble at Hawkstone Park.

12.4.57   Pictures: "Wooden Horse".

15.4.57   Wendy the goat had Billy twins.

20.4 57   Pictures: "The Crowd Roars".

25.4 57   Evans the Mill bought 5 store pigs. £36.

27.4.57   Fire Patrol Cownwy Valley.

2.5.57   Sowed wheat at Brynheddyn.

| | |
|---|---|
| 3.5.57 | Pictures: "Tarzan and his Mate". |
| 4.5.57 | Went to see cup final at Brynawl. On TV. |
| 6.5.57 | Mother bought 25 three month old pullets. 10/- each. |
| 17.5.57 | Pictures: "Seven Brides for Seven Brothers". |
| 24.5.57 | Pictures: "The Gentle Gunman". |
| 31.5.57 | Pictures: "The Last Command". |
| 1.6.57 | Dad and Phillip started to slate cow shed roof. |
| 10.6.57 | Whit Monday motor cycle racing at Oulton Park. |
| 13.6.57 | Started to work saw brashing with Emyr Lloyds gang in Cownwy Valley. |
| 15.6.57 | Went to Pen-y-bont-fawr show. |
| 16.6.57 | Phillip took mother, auntie Marie and Kath to Fairbourne. |
| 18.7.57 | Had first cheque for 8 lambs. £43-4-3d. |
| 20.7.57 | Went to Liverpool Show. |
| 24.7.57 | Wool went away by Rail. |
| 5.8.57 | Went to Whitchurch Show. |
| 10.8.57 | Had money for wool. £17-3s. |
| 24.5.57 | Sold bullock at home for £50. |
| 28.5.57 | Sold 14 young pigs in Oswestry. £79-16s. |
| 31.5.57 | Bought first TV set. |
| 7.9.57 | Went to Blackpool for the day. |
| 13.9.57 | Pictures started again. "All for Mary". |
| 18.9.57 | Sold 8 ewes for £4 each and bought an in-pig gelt. £41. |
| 20.9.57 | Pictures: "Knights of the Round Table". |
| 21.9.57 | LCWW ewe sale. Bought 11 lambs. £27-10s. |
| 28.9.57 | Pictures: "The Love Match". |
| 29.9.57 | Cut and stacked Wheat Field. |
| 3.10.57 | Carried the Wheat. |
| 4.10.57 | Pictures: "Trouble in the Glen". |
| 11.10.57 | Pictures: "Value for Money". |
| 14.10.57 | Sold 18 cockerels. £9-16s. |
| 18.10.57 | Pictures: "The Road to Denver". |
| 25.10.57 | Pictures: "The Time of Your Life". |
| 28.10.57 | Shot partridge at Cefn. |
| 29.10.57 | Poppy Whist at the Lake. |
| 1.11.57 | Pictures: "Quo Vardis". Phillip took mother to see |

auntie Eva in Yorkshire.

| | |
|---|---|
| 3.11.57 | Bishop of St Asaph came to Hirnant Church. |
| 7.11.57 | Came off motor cycle on way to work. |
| 8.11.57 | Went to SOH with crack in my shoulder. All ill with Flu. |
| 15.11.57 | Pictures: "The Bounty Hunters". |
| 16.11.57 | Went with Maldwyn on the bus to watch Wolves 1 - West Brom 1. Pictures: "The Gun Fight at OK Corral". |
| 19.11.57 | Church Whist at the Lake. |
| 22.11.57 | Pictures: "See How They Run". |
| 25.11.57 | First day in hospital, shoulder. |
| 29.11.57 | Home for the weekend. |
| 30.11.57 | Home after electric treatment. |
| 5.12.57 | Pictures: "Carry on Admiral". |
| 12.12.57 | Finished at the Hospital. |
| 17.12.57 | Thrashing the wheat at Brynheddyn. |
| 23.12.57 | Grey Ferge. Whist drive in Hirnant school. |
| 27.12.57 | Pictures: "Young at Heart". |

*A short reply to a RSPB report*

Regarding what the RSPB are doing on the Estate Farm at the moment. Let us not forget what the Liverpool Corporation Farm did in the past.

In the early days the estate was self supporting and more organic than the RSPB will ever be. In the early 50s I can remember the farm growing swedes, mangels and potatoes, cutting corn and hay with the binder etc. The fertilizer was good old farmyard muck, not Nitros etc., what has been used and ruined the land by the Severn Trent management. Also every man on the estate was allowed to plant potatoes and carrots along with the estate crops, but this perk came to an end in the 60s or 70s.

As regards to being organic, I do not believe any farm on a large scale can be fully organic, too many loop holes and paper work, plus fiddles. If any farm can be organic, Llechwedd-Du can with what we keep, but it is only a fad.

I agree with what cattle the RSPB are keeping, and as things are going, I think we will all be going back to native breeds and continentals will be phased out. Give it ten years and you will see the change.

Regarding indoor lambing, I see this as a waste of time and money. OK if you keep cross-bred ewes, like Suffolk, Mules, Texels, etc., but Welsh and speckle is a waste of time. Native breeds lamb much better natural, in the open fields. The margin of profit is nil if you take into account labour and extra feed, more losses. In-door lambing is a twenty-four hour job, OK if you work for yourself but if you have to employ labour and pay overtime you will be losing money, even if you get good subsidies.

Let's not forget what went on in the past when as I understand eleven to thirteen thousand sheep were kept on the hills in the early days when lambs were kept for two to three years before being sold. Shearing by hand, twenty to thirty shearers and being paid peanuts, but they all loved their job.

I was brought up within a mile of fen country, namely Brown Moss and Fenn's Bank running through to Whixhall Moss.

Peat was a supplement to the smallholder in this area and was sold for fuel in the towns and villages. Each Friday a horse and cart loaded with peat blocks would call at each house in the street selling it by the sackful, working out at the 1945/50 years at 6d a block. Deep peat, which was dark chocolate colour was hard and lasted longer, surface peat was a lighter colour but bigger blocks and was used as fire lighters. Mother would have two bags a week because coal was on ration. The only trouble with peat as a fuel was it was very dusty and if you had a blow back down the chimney you would have some dusting to do.

As you travelled on the train from Whitchurch to Oswestry you passed through Fenn's Bank and Whixhall Moss and each holding would have its stacks of peat. The Moss was common land and each holding joining to the Moss had peat rights. It was firstly cut and left to dry on the side of the dyke. After it was dry it was moved with a small sledge pulled by a light horse to a stack with airways running through the stack and was left to dry for three years, selling the older stacks first. It was a lovely sight to see the straight lines of the dykes and perfect stacks of peat blocks as you looked through the train windows. Special tools were made for the job and this was done by the local blacksmith.

There is no alternative for peat for the gardener and nursery man, that is why Irish Moss Peat is imported, because the Irish have had little interference from the government so far. Peat is big business in Ireland. Peat free compost is useless in many ways.

Your plants get too waterlogged. Pure peat is weed free and others are too sour for many plants. Agriculture and forestry always seem to get the blame. Farmers have land and have to make full use of it. It's no use having cold wet land, that is why it has to be drained. The same goes for forestry. That is only what the land is good for.

Brown Moss is just on the outskirts of Whitchurch and when we were children Mother would take us to Brown Moss for a picnic. It was lovely and unspoilt then but now it is a real dump. I took June, Ian and Antonette for a ride there after we were married and old forty-five gallon oil drums, old cars, bicycles, etc., had been dumped in the water. So different when we were young — a haven for pond life, birds and insects.

I was walking across the Moss one spring day and disturbed a skylark from her nest in the marshy grass. Four eggs she had and they had scribble like marking on the eggs. Quite large eggs for the size of the bird. Dragonflies and damselflies in abundance. Carp were the fish in the pool, they like dark murky water and the anglers would always fish at night. As we got older we used to go to the Moss after school in the summer evenings and watch the hawk moths flying around just before dark. These are the biggest of the British moth family, around two and a half to three inches and lovely colours. What I cannot understand is this — why was there more wildlife around in those days when there was no law against catching butterflies, collecting birds' eggs, etc.?

Don't blame the farmers, blame the predators such as hawks, foxes, badgers, grey squirrels, minks and polecats to name a few, and until they are culled you will find a decline in wildlife of every kind. Let's keep a balance not breed hawks etc., to be let free to do more damage.

I have always had a craze on 'Fancy' poultry. I am not keen on modern fowl bred just for egg production but more of the rare breeds type.

Now my first recollection of poultry must have been when Mother bought me six Kaki Cambell ducklings from Whitchurch market when I was ill with my leg just after the war. I remember bringing in these little ducklings and putting them in a little box by the fire. Mother went into the garden and what did I do but to fill the sink with water and let the little ducks have a swim around the sink. Mother came in and I got a telling off because I didn't know that, if little ducks got very wet too young, they would get too wet and cold and die. We did lose one but the rest lived for a number of years. Dad made a run for them at the bottom of the garden and they laid very well. I used to go into the run and dig worms for them. I stuck the fork through my foot, also through one of the duck's webbed feet and she always had a hole through her foot for the rest of her life.

Dad bought a big shed off a neighbour. Eighteen feet by six feet I think it was. After that he bought twelve battery cages for twelve Light Sussex Brown Leghorn pullets. Now this was great because I was in charge of these hens. After a while Arthur printed cards to put in front of each feeding trough. These cards were to record each hen's egg production, this went on for a while. Each hen was numbered from 1 to 12, if a hen didn't average five eggs per week she had to go and be replaced by another pullet until we had twelve good hens going. Arthur then made a further fifteen battery cages so as to fill the rest of the shed space.

Mother and Dad used to talk a lot about the poultry they kept when they were young. Mother talked about Barnett hens, which were not a breed as such but chickens bred by a Mr Barnett, but Mother called them Barnett fowl. These were the first hens they kept after they married in the 1920s, she recalled how they used to lay in the flower borders right near the house and used to lay an egg, round like a table tennis ball. Dad talked about poultry that his mother kept, old breeds which are now classed as rare breeds and fetch big money today, some breeds £60 to £70 per pair.

Grandmother used to walk to the market like most farmer's wives did with eggs, butter, etc., some four to five miles each Friday with a basket laden with produce. This was the only way to sell at the turn of the century.

My grandfather always kept and milked Shorthorn cattle which were the main breed kept until the war in 1939. Butter and cheese were made and sold in the markets and surplus milk and whey was fed to the pigs and calves. Shorthorn cattle had a far higher butterfat content than the modern Friesian Holstean cattle but less volume of milk. In milk sold in the early days, you could see the cream through the bottle but today it is more like watered down milk.

We moved to Wales in 1951, brought the battery cages with us and after we bought Brynheddyn these were erected in the old dairy and we kept Light Sussex cockerels in them to fatten for Christmas. We caponised these birds to get them bigger and fatter, this was done by injecting a small hormone pellet into the back of the head. It is illegal to do this today, but a breed has been developed today called the Cob, bred for quick and early development. I had them up to 14lb each last Christmas. After we moved to Pen-y-Geuffordd we had erected a big deep litter and kept around 150 birds, mainly Light Sussex Brown Leghorn.

After we moved to Brwynen in 1964 I got into poultry more, by keeping ducks, geese, pheasants, peafowl, guinea fowl, turkeys and even tried quail. I have also kept pigeons. We once bought some Indian Runner ducks off Vernon Jackson, Llanrhaeadr a big duck breeder at the time, let them out, they went into the brook and we lost some down the culvert.

When John Wiblyn was our forester I had the job of going round the gangs with him because he had not passed his driving test. One day I had to go to Oswestry in the van and called at the dentist on the way home. John came with me to Brwynen with his daughter Shana as I had a hen hatching three peafowl eggs and wanted the little girl to watch. The three did hatch, two hens and one cock bird. The peacock went on to be a beautiful bird, his tail when spread must have been five to six foot across. He lived for quite a number of years but was very noisy in the spring, starting to call at 4 a.m. and kept it up all day.

Turkeys were bred and hatched for Christmas sales, so were geese. The stag turkey we had was very savage and used to wait by the gate for Kath to come home from school with Ted Hill and chase and peck her legs, so did the gander one time.

I bred hundreds of pheasants for the late John Ransford, for his shoots at Bishop's Castle.

Before I married I bought a big shed thirty feet by fifteen feet, for keeping and breeding dogs but I now keep poultry in this shed. I am now into fancy fowl and have bought a new shed for incubation and rearing the young birds. The breeds I have to date are Light Sussex bantam miniature game, Pekin bantams, Silver Seabrights, Large Fowl Cockins, German Appenzeller Spitzharvens, Polish Frazzels, Buff Rock bantams and Speckeldys. I have started to show poultry and eggs. Two firsts and a third with eggs at Llanfyllin Show. A first, second and third with four birds at the Oswestry Poultry Show in September.

It has not been a very good breeding year, too cold and wet, causing a lot of infertile eggs. Quite a number of birds I have not bred from yet, but I am looking forward to the spring. Cochin's are the breed I want to specialise in because they come in a range of colours from White, Buff, Cuckoo, Blues, and Blacks and have feathered legs. I crossed my five black and one white hen with a blue cock and all the birds turned out blue, bar one big white cock so I am now up to around forty Cochins.

My first job when I was as young as ten years old was with the Crewe Co-op, Whitchurch branch. My brothers, Arthur and Phillip handed the job down as they left school.

I was working with a local man who moved with his work to live in Crewe. Harry Wilkinson was his name, quite a character, I must admit. A man who could not care less about anybody and was very outspoken. I think a bit rubbed off onto me. Harry would bring a load of goods and bread, five days a week, from Crewe to the Whitchurch shop. Customers' orders would then be loaded into Harry's van, along with the bread.

For around eighteen months after starting work I was still going to junior school in the town. Harry would arrive outside the school at around 3.45 p.m. with his old Morris Commercial van with a klaxon horn which Harry would blow three times just to annoy the headmaster. The headmaster would look over his glasses and give me a dirty look because he knew Harry was waiting for me.

Monday evenings were spent delivering bread around the town, which would take until around 6 p.m. Harry would then take me home, then give me half a crown (2/6 or 12½p) and a loaf of bread for Mum and then go back to Crewe for his tea. Tuesday evening we went round the villages of Ash, Ightfield, Calverhall and Broughall, where my father's brothers farmed. This was mostly orders of groceries as well as bread. Thursdays were the same but the villages of Bronington, Fenn's Bank, Bettisfield and Iscoed. Fridays were the Malpas area villages. Saturdays were spent a full morning around the town.

My pay was 2/6 for an evening and 5/- (25p) for a Saturday morning. I was not paid by the Co-op but by Harry for helping him. He paid me each evening with half a crown and Saturday morning with two half a crowns and I always gave my mother half.

Now during the holidays I spent most days working with Harry for 5/- a day, making a total of £1 5s, also a loaf a day as well. As I got older and went to the senior school at Broughall I had my own customers and made many friends.

Harry was popular with the ladies and I had to sit and wait for him for quite a while sometimes. I remember waiting one time at the top of Belton Road in the town. We had a new van, and I was sitting in the van getting fed up and starting to fiddle with things in the van and let the handbrake off. The van set off down the road and had gone eight or ten yards down the road before I managed to put the brake back on. Harry came out of the house and never noticed the van had moved.

I remember one time Harry had a customer in Ash, and this lady who knew my mother well, had a young Light Sussex cockerel which Harry used to tease. This cockerel got savage and used to fly at Harry and jump on him and peck his back. What did Harry do but give this customer to me. I had short trousers and an iron leg, and sure enough he used to have me just as I got to the gate. I got fed up of this and one Tuesday I went round and she had left a bread bin with a note inside, "Two loaves please", this was my chance to get my own back. I put the bread in the bin and picked up a garden cane and walked calmly to the gate and sure enough he came round the corner of the house and ran after me and had a go at me. I nobbled him at the back of his neck and left him flapping on the floor. I never saw him again (perhaps she sold him — joke!). I never told Harry, but this lady told my mother about this cockerel dying by the gate. Mother said, "What a shame."

In the winter of 47 we had a lot of snow in Whitchurch, not as bad as in Llanwddyn as I understand from Jack Carsley, but the worst winter we had before we moved to Wales. Around Whitchurch we had a number of airfields and they had big blowers for clearing snow off the runways. Well I think the council hired them off the RAF to clear the country roads. I say the country roads because they were like big vacuum cleaners on the front of the lorry and sucked up the snow and blew it over the hedge into the fields. Just bad luck if you were the other side of the hedge or had a nice garden to flatten with snow.

I worked with Harry for close on five years and never remember him breaking down or getting stuck in the snow. He put chains on his back wheels in bad weather and they helped a lot but the ride in the van was very rough.

I was quite interested in football by now and Harry was a big Crewe Alexandria supporter. About once a month Harry would take me back to Crewe with him, have dinner, then take me to see the Alex play. I remember in 1948, Crewe were drawn at home to Derby County, they in the old Division 1. Harry managed to get tickets and Derby won 1-0 with a crowd of 18,000. This was in the FA Cup. After the match Harry would take me to Crewe Station and see me off on the train home.

Getting back to working with the Co-op — around Christmas time it was good working with Harry because most of the customers gave you a Christmas tip. I used to get enough tip money to buy all my family and friends a Christmas present.

During the summer holidays I used to like delivering around Prees and Prees Heath where the old airfield was during the war. Firstly we had to take the goods to the Prees branch and have a tea break. There was a lady who worked in the shop who knew my mother and she gave me an aniseed cake to take home, but during the day I kept taking bits of the cake until it had all gone. I never told my mother, but I did have a bellyache later.

Next stop was the Breakland Cafe and Raven Hotel at Prees Heath where we had to take big long loaves to go in the slicing machines. We always had a dinner at the Raven Hotel

After finishing with Harry to leave school in 1949, Harry himself finished with the Co-op and went as an insurance man in Crewe.

I left school in July 1949 and spent my last school holidays working most days for Whitchurch Co-op, delivering bread and goods to all the outlying villages and the town. By now Harry had a new Austin van and I felt quite a chap travelling around in this new van. Sitting in the van waiting for Harry, I got a bit bored, we were at the top of the town, Belton Road it was, on a bit of a slope. What did I do but let the handbrake off. So off we sail down the road, no cars outside the houses like today, but went about twenty yards down the middle of the road before I managed to pull the handbrake back on; blocking all the traffic and having a telling off when Harry did come back to his van

I had worked for the Co-op since I was ten as I have told you in an earlier story about Harry picking me up from school. Now fifteen I had had a job for five years, not bad to think I was still only fifteen years old.

In September 1949 Mother sent me to a YMCA work-seeking centre at Hinstock near Market Drayton some twelve miles from Whitchurch. This was an eight week course. First week was spent working in the hostel. This entailed cleaning the dormitories, making beds and preparing veg in the kitchen. This was a laugh because they had a machine for cleaning the potatoes which was very good but I was a little bit too clever. I hate peeling onions, so after a day or two peeling a net of onions I decided to put them in the potato machine. Big onions in, spring onions out. I only did it once. I don't know why!

The second week was the start of my farming life and after fifty years I'm still doing my best to keep going. I was lucky, I went to a farm at Cheswardine, next village to Hinstock. I went on my bicycle each morning. I worked for a Mr and Mrs Price and family on a farm called Mount Pleasant; a family who knew my father's family very well. What a great seven weeks, working five days per week, riding home on a Friday after work and riding back to the YMCA Sunday afternoon.

This was a big sandstone farm, perhaps some of the best ground in Shropshire. You could grow owt! It was now mid September 1949. This was where I learnt to milk by hand, milking two beef shorthorn cows with the stockman night and morning. Beef shorthorn cows were kept and crossed with a Hereford bull. The calves were all bucket fed and were finished with a home-mixed feed. Good cattle but would be too fat for today's market.

Mr Price would always bring the cattle in each afternoon, the only work I saw him do in fact. The cows were always first and I always remember the fat old Hereford bull at the rear with Mr Price's daughter riding on his back and his arm over the bull's rump. A sight you never see today. Herefords were the main bull in the 50s until the continentals took over in the 70s, but I think the native breeds will be back within ten years because of the feeding costs, plus organic farming coming into the fore. Mount Pleasant was mainly arable, growing sugar beet, grain and field beans. Mr Price employed a stock man and a tractor driver but they helped each other for the milking.

Picture a twenty acre field with an oak wood down three sides, plus the main road down the fourth side. Well this field was sown with field beans and that was my first job, on the platform of the seed drill, making sure the drill was kept full. The tractor was a big blue Fordson Major, the one that came after the Ford Standard. The field was then harrowed and rolled. The following day I was picking docks into sacks off another field being prepared for winter barley, what a boring job.

I had never been told that a shooting syndicate from Birmingham had the contract of shooting pigeons for the next three days. Pigeons as I now understand are very fond of field beans. All this bang, bang, bang all day, I thought it was an army manoeuvre. The second day I was allowed to watch the shoot for an hour or so with Mr Price shooting as well for a day's sport. The syndicate started in the morning, about twenty guns; firstly they would put up a hide and then put out in the field decoys like pigeons, some on the ground like feeding, others on sticks with wings as if landing.

Into the hide and wait for the birds to arrive. The pigeons came down onto the field in droves. They were shot mostly before getting onto the field. The birds were so stupid they seemed to fly from one side of the field to the other guns after they had been shot at. There were that many of them, nearly 2,000 birds were shot in three days, then each afternoon they would be loaded into vans and taken to Birmingham. After three or so days the beans would start to grow, then the pigeons would not eat them.

Mount Pleasant looked onto Tern Hill Air Base and I loved to watch the planes taking off and landing. Havards and Percival Prentices were the fighter planes. This was a base for training fighter pilots. 1949 was not long after the war and so Tern Hill was in full swing. Not so far from Tern Hill base was Shawbury the bomber training base with Lancasters and Avro Hansens. Phillip was an electrician at this time on the Lancasters at Shawbury. Round Mount Pleasant planes could be seen and heard all the day, the sky seemed full of planes.

The buildings being sandstone built were very bad for rats; rat holes in the sandstone walls. Mr Price had two Jack Russell terriers and they seemed very placid family pets. One big bay of barley had not been thrashed and in one side of the bay was a big hole made by the rats to move from the bay to the farm buildings. One afternoon the thrashing and stationary bailer arrived and was set up ready for thrashing the next morning. While we were milking, the tractor driver and two men with the thrashing box erected netting around the bay.

Thrashing started around 10 a.m. and I could understand why Mr and Mrs Price kept the two Jack Russells because about a quarter way down the bay the rats started to be uncovered and run out. One terrier on the bay the other outside waiting for rats to cross to the buildings. You couldn't beat a good day's thrashing for a good day's sport sloshing rats. I was pitching to the platform on the box, so had to uncover the rats under the sheaves. The more you went down the bay the more rats there were. The terrier on the bay was all bitten around the nose but this made him more savage. The rats were hanging to his lip and nose as he tried to shake them. The dead rats were everywhere because as the dog killed them I had to throw them off the bay with the pitchfork out of the way. The terrier outside was having rats also, the ones that tried to make it to the buildings. Mr Price did not have a lot of barley out of this bay, the rats had a good share.

The next day I had to collect the rats in the wheelbarrow and bury them. I did start to count them as I loaded them into the barrow but lost count.

I finished working for Mr and Mrs Price, Mount Pleasant late November 1949 and had a very good reference from them.

In January 1950 I started my first job with pay through the YMCA I might add, with a Mr and Mrs Joe Oliver, Field Farm, Agden, near Malpas, Cheshire, not too far from home.

In January 1950 I started my first job with proper wages. Through the YMCA I had a job with a Mr and Mrs Joe Oliver, Field Agden, Nr Malpas, not far from my home in Whitchurch but I had to live in.

This was where I found out about pedigree animals because Mr Oliver kept and bred pedigree dairy shorthorn cattle and pedigree large white pigs and he used to show both. We milked with a 2-milk unit Fullwood milking machine and each cow's milk was recorded twice a day.

Shorthorn colours range from dark red, red and white, roan and white. One red and white cow I became very fond of, and I think she was the only one who I remember the name of, it was Agden Wild Eyes.

Field farm was around eighty acres but very good land in Cheshire. Mr Oliver milked around twenty to twenty-five cows, but the milk was very high in butter fat, much higher than in today's Friesians. Each morning, Mrs Oliver would go to the dairy with a jug and skim the previous afternoon's churns and fill the jug with cream. While I worked for Mr Oliver I never remember having milk in my coffee, always cream, a treat on its own.

Mr Oliver didn't show his cattle the year I worked for him but he did his pigs. One good sow he took round the shows was Agden Molly Baines, a good sow with plenty of length and carried herself well. I went with Mr Oliver to two shows in the summer of 1950, Lymm in Cheshire and Oswestry Show. I travelled in the back of the lorry with the pigs to make sure they kept clean.

Not so much work getting pigs ready for showing as our Highland cattle, no brushing and combing. We just gave them a wash and scrub and put white sawdust flour on their backs before showing.

When you show pigs you walk them around the ring with a patter, a flat stick supplied by meal companies. Mr Oliver used one with Silcocks printed on it. For boars, you had a board made with a hole through for your hand and this was used in the same manner but in front of the pig's face so as not to see the other boars or you would have a fight on your hands.

Mr Oliver had pig arks out in the fields for the sows with litters. Each sow would go round the field with her litter but would sleep in her own ark. When you keep pigs you always keep rats as well and they lived under the arks, so this was the job from time to time, move the ark with the David Brown, a couple of good terriers and a good day's sport was had by all. The arks were moved but the rats had set up home and burrowed into the ground like rabbits. Mr Oliver must have been used to this because he had a length of pipe which he attached to the exhaust of the tractor and put it up the rat holes, started up the tractor and gassed the little beggars out. Out they would come but the terriers made quick work of them.

Silage was made as well as hay but so different than today. We made it in round stacks. Cut and carried loose grass every other day, a hard job because green grass is very heavy to load and unload. Black treacle was diluted and poured over each layer, this was how silage was made in the 40s and 50s.

Now the next-door neighbour, a Mr Simister, he made dried grass meal and baled. This was done by contractors, Cheshire Farmers took it on lorries to their Mill in Grinley Brook and brought it back to the farm. The fields were cut three times in the summer but it only had to be ten to twelve inches in height and all leaf no seed head.

Mr Simister also kept pedigree cattle, Blue Albion was the breed and they are now on the list of rare breeds. They are very much like the Friesians but blue and white not black and white. I think it was the Friesian that finished the Albion off because

E

they gave more milk.

Mr and Mrs Oliver were a religious family, they were Plymouth Brethren and had services in their own home around the piano. I never remember the Oliver family use a swear word or lose their temper. The meals were great, coffee was drunk, not tea, coffee made in a percolator and made with cream. Each morning of the week you had an egg cooked differently.

Hay was made loose before the pick-up baler came out. Rowing in with a hay rake before cocking the hay with the old wooden hay rake. I got blisters in the middle of my right hand which went septic and I had to go and have it lanced by the doctor in Whitchurch, and had two weeks off work When I did go back to work, hay harvest had finished and pig shows had started. Most of the shows Mr Oliver went to on his own with car and trailer.

Most of the work I had to do was to milk morning and night. Mr Oliver did all the feeding, I did the mucking out of the pigs. One sow I hated, she used to bite the brush. I used to help Mr Oliver tattoo the pigs and calves, also hold the little pigs while he castrated them.

My last job with Mr Oliver was to help thrash a bay of barley and this job I always liked because I used to help Farmer Luton when I was at school, but that's another story.

Getting back to work, my job was to thread the wires through the stationary baler. This was done by threading wires through two needles between each bale. An old tramp used to go round with this box bagging the chaff at the end of the box. This tramp's name was Harry Dodd and he lived in an old railway container in the fields at Grinley Brook. Now this old tramp collected the rats after thrashing and picked out the best rat and was taking it home to roast for Sunday dinner. He was going to grill it over an open fire outside his shack.

Sadly my job came to an end because my ankle started to go wrong after the operation I had in 1948. I had a lot of pain trying to put my boots on in the mornings. My foot had started to turn over making me walk on the side of my foot. I could not carry on with all the pain. I had to leave work and go into the

SOH in November 1950. This operation was to lock my ankle up again, and this is how I am today.

When I came out of hospital, just before Christmas 1950, Mother started to look for a smallholding for sale and we ended up buying Pen-y-Geuffordd in Hirnant, and we moved in on 21st March 1951, just fifty years ago, and I was still on the sick when we moved into Pen-y-Geuffordd after my new operation.

On March 21st 1951 we moved to Wales, the most wonderful time of my life. We moved from a council house in Whitchurch to the very rural village of Hirnant.

Mother had saved all she could to try and buy a smallholding anywhere, to try and get into the country, to live and do what we liked best. Mother used to buy the *Smallholder*, a paper that advertised smallholdings etc. Dad didn't really want to move from Whitchurch because it meant leaving all his family and work mates, but I suppose he was outnumbered. Phillip, Margaret and myself were teenagers and wanted to move.

We all put our savings together and bought Pen-y-Geuffordd, the old family home of the Hughes (Ted, Harry, etc.). We went by taxi to see the holding, just Mother, Dad and me, and Mother and me fell in love with Pen-y-Geuffordd at first sight. A Mr and Mrs Atkinson owned it then, it was arranged that I go to stay for a week to see how I would like it, because at that time Phillip was serving ten years in the RAF and Margaret, my sister was a nanny in Brighton. My mother was hoping that it would be just Dad, myself and Mum moving to Wales because Pen-y-Geuffordd was a one up, one down, a back kitchen and a box room. But things didn't turn out quite right, but that's another story.

As I said, I spent a week at Pen-y-Geuffordd and it was great catching rabbits and going for long walks. We bought Pen-y-Geuffordd in March 1951 for £1,650, this was for the holding, stock and small farm tools. Mr and Mrs Atkinson moved out on March 21st in the morning and we moved in the same afternoon with the fire still burning. We had two lorry loads of furniture etc., and we were finished before dark.

I remember feeding the stock while Dad and Phil unloaded the furniture. There were two sows and a litter of eight pigs, twelve ducks and about fifty hens, three cats and a pot-bellied Friesian heifer calf. I collected eight duck eggs and a number of hens eggs so we had a breakfast at least.

The first night we slept on mattresses on the big bedroom floor. Of course in the fifties there was no electricity in the valley so we had to manage with oil lamps for three years, a change from Whitchurch. A couple of days passed and we had the place shipshape.

We had no running water so we had to collect water in a bucket from a spring down by the river, we also had an outside toilet which was a pain in the neck. After a while Phillip and Dad sunk a well just below the house and put a semi-rotary pump over the sink in the back kitchen which was still used when we moved to Brwynen twelve years later.

Phillip was stationed at RAF Shawbury and came home on his old Sunbeam motorbike at weekends, but was soon moved to Germany. I was lucky really because I got a job in the village on the following Monday after moving, with Glyn and Vera Humphreys at Llan Farm. This was wonderful, like going back in time. Every farm still had a team of Shire horses and Glyn was very good with Shires as I remember. He had a lovely black mare who always did well at Pen-y-bont-fawr show.

Dad had more difficulty getting work because he was in his mid-fifties. He did try for a job with the Liverpool Corporation but Mr Howard told him he was looking for younger men. After a while Mr Quine did get him a job with Gordon's, the only sub-contractor firm on the estate at that time. He worked with Dai Revel, Jack Tan-Bwlch, Doug Buttery, Sid Watkins, etc. This was slave labour and nearly killed my poor old dad. The work was very hard, loading timber by hand, rolling timber up skids onto lorries. He got hurt many times and ended up in hospital more than once. He lasted a couple of years and ended up with arthritis.

Working with Glyn and Huw Jones from Hen Dafarn was so different, milking ten cows night and morning with a Simplex milking machine, driven by a petrol Lister hopper cooled stationary engine. This was OK when it was working, or if Glyn had any petrol, half the time we milked by hand. The milk was collected each morning by Vaggs of Nesscliff off a stand by the dairy. John Jones came down each day from Blaen Hirnant, with churns behind his Allis Charmers row crop tractor and Dick Wynn would come all the way from Brynheddyn in an old converted Austin 7 — they were good days. I learnt to plough with an old Ford Standard tractor and a Lister Cockshut trailer plough.

The school had three children, Eryl, Glyndwr, Blaen Hirnant and Iola Bwlchsych, a teacher Miss Griffiths, Hen Dafarn and a cook Miss Jenkins, Clochnant Bach.

On Wednesday morning (which we called Farmer's Sunday) a Crossville bus would come to the village, turn round by Llan and pick up as many as eight people to go shopping to Oswestry. Mother would go one week and Dad the next. Things were still on ration then. The road from Hirnant to Pen-y-bont-fawr was narrower then than it is now and if the bus met the milk lorry there was nearly a fight between the bus conductor and the lorry driver because they fell out about who was to give way and reverse, nearly always by Ty-Brith.

There were nearly 100 people living in Hirnant in the early fifties. A service was held in the church each Sunday afternoon, Ben Jones would ring the bell. And the chapel, which is now a house in Pen-y-bont-fawr had two services each Sunday and sometimes three. Whist drives were held in the school. I once won 'lowest score gents' there, which was a brace of rabbits. Bob Jerkins from the vicarage was the roadman who took a pride in his work not like today! Mrs Lewis ran the village shop, a sister to Glyn Humphries, so was Tom Evans' wife from Bwlchsych. Ben Jones from Bryn-Awel would walk to the village each morning. He was a very good singer and he would sing all the way to the village.

I loved Pen-y-Geuffordd and the village that much, I never

went from the village for two years. It was just the three of us at this time and we were nearly self supporting. We had a very good garden which had been rested for many years and grew all our own veg. Shot, snared, ferreted many rabbits. Killed a pig each year. Dad and Mother made butter, we had two cows by now so had plenty of milk. Cream for the butter and Dad loved buttermilk and all the spare went to the pigs and calves.

Our family moved to Wales on 21st March 1952, the first day of spring, a lovely dry day with snow still on the hills where it had drifted.

Things got off to a good start with animals to feed and water. One sow had eight young pigs which had been ordered before we moved to Pen-y-Geuffordd, these had to be collected or delivered when ready and they had been sold for £8 each, as much or more than they are making today.

When the sows needed service they had to be taken to Evans' the Mill, Pen-y-bont-fawr, a day's job as I remember. You either tied a rope to one of the pig's back legs or she walked OK. It was quite a nice job meeting people and having a chat along the way to give yourself a rest (and the pig as well). Job done, then the return journey after paying Glyn or Mr Evans £1 for the service. This was OK until you took a gilt who had never been to the Mill before, making her go along the road with a stick to smack her to make her go or a clout on the snout if she tried to go back home or met a car. It was a hard job but we were never beaten.

Same with the cows to visit the bull. Mr Gwilym Evans, Cymur, it was then, he had a ministry bull, a big Red Hereford, not quite so far as the Pen-y-bont-fawr (£1 per cow).

We did have one cow who went on her own and when ready, Gwilym would put her through the gate and she would return home.

In the early days Edwin Hughes, Clochnant, had the rabbit contract at Llan and he used to snare, trap and ferret the rabbits and he caught loads. The traps were placed down the holes and when the rabbits came in or out they would be caught by the back or front leg. These traps are banned now, they were very cruel.

All the ground around Pen-y-Geuffordd belonged to Llan and when we came to the holding we took on three cats, a tabby, a black and one white and I am afraid they didn't last very long. The tabby came home dragging the trap, caught by her front leg and only held by the skin. Dad cut the leg off and bandaged it up and she managed OK until she went again and we never saw her again.

The black one went missing, caught in traps we believe. Now the white one was a different tale, I think she was used to sleeping in the oven. I suppose some readers can put two and two together and know what happened. Mother shut the oven door and lit the fire and when the oven started to warm up the cat started to move about and jump inside the oven, rattling the bars. Mother opened the door and out jumps a ginger cat never to be seen again!

We were left with a pot-bellied Friesian heifer about six months old who had been fed on potato peelings etc., not much hay I think. We bought our first cow off Dai Dairy. I think she must have been fifty years old. Denis Glanrhyd walked her to Pen-y-Geuffordd and took the little Friesian back; I don't recall how much the bargain was. We could not get the old Welsh Black in calf, so she was taken to Welshpool and sold for £25, but Dad did buy a lovely roan Hereford for £50 and that was the our first good cow. My uncle Ted gave us a set of twin Friesian heifers and uncle Fred gave Dad a blue Friesian heifer, that is how we started with cattle.

A few years later the Rev Hopkin Evans was the vicar in Llanwddyn and not married at the time and Dad used to go to church in Hirnant. Hopkin didn't know my dad but ended up at Pen-y-Geuffordd for tea and bought one of the Friesian heifers and I bought two ewes and four lambs off the vicar. The deals were made but no money changed hands until Jack Lloyd Waen delivered the ewes and lambs and took the heifer back. Hopkin's ewes were our first sheep. The blue heifer of uncle Fred was sold to John Jones, Blind-Hirnant for £100 after she had her first calf.

Phillip had gone to Germany to serve his time in the RAF. This was how Mother wanted it really because the house was so small.

Mother ordered a nanny goat kid from a Mrs Mostyn Owen, a big goat breeder in Derbyshire. Mother collected the goat from Oswestry Station one Wednesday when she had gone to town. She bought the little kid home on the bus and it bleated all the way because it wanted a bottle of milk. This little goat grew up to give a lot of milk in her time, but she was also a demon as well. Mother used to wash Dad's and my socks and hang them on the fence. Wendy as she was called would chew all the feet off the socks and leave them lying about the yard. I used to take her with me to work when I was spreading muck, by hand in those days ( I mean with a fork of course!).

At dinner time I would pass Hirnant Post Office and village shop. A Mr and Mrs Orrit ran the Post Office until 1956. I remember calling into the shop for some treacle toffee and sure enough Wendy came into the shop. Below the counter hung National Savings Posters etc. Wendy took a fancy to the posters and started ripping them down and eating them. Mr Orrit just stood there with his mouth open. Wendy liked treacle toffee and I used to laugh at her getting them stuck in her teeth. I remember being with her, spreading muck on the 14th May — Bala Fair, Tommy Davies passing through the village with a load to Bala and it was snowing very heavy but wet snow.

It must have been around 1953 when things started to move. Phillip had been bought out of the RAF and Kathleen was born. My grandfather had died and left Dad some money in his will. But as there were six sons to share the will it was not a lot, but we did manage to buy Brynheddyn on the Cefn Road and rent ten acres of woodland from Mr Robert Cefn. By renting Cefn wood we were able to join the holdings and make one unit. We had enough cattle but we started to buy more sheep.

As a lifelong lover of birds before the RSPB came along, I often get to wonder if the RSPB are doing a good job or not!

Is it a good thing to protect all birds of prey? You read in the papers and on TV about the increase of these vicious birds in Wales, some bred in captivity and released into the wild. Surely, soon you will be asking farmers and game keepers to control them again. We hear of the decrease in the smaller bird population, surely common sense tells you that an imbalance of birds of prey, crows, magpies, jays, etc., are the main cause of the decline. I am very observant when I go about the countryside, I have seen a sparrow hawk take a swallow, falcons taking pigeons and a goshawk taking my chickens, and I bet a buzzard will take lambs as well. Crows, magpies and jays will take eggs and young birds, and so will grey squirrels, so our young birds will not have a chance.

We hear of our estate being a nature reserve, is this a good thing? No! Surely birds need peace and quiet at nesting time. I know from experience if you mess about with birds at nesting time they will forsake their nest and you cannot blame the poor little birds if kids and adults are watching them and poking fingers into the nests all the while. As I have said before, birds need solitude in the spring but to encourage more twitchers onto the estate will spoil the reserve, as simple as that.

I can tell you this, there were more birds around from the 50s to 80s than there are today because they need to be left alone and controlled properly.

Pen-y-Geuffordd overlooked Hirnant Church across the valley. What a peaceful place to live, going back in time as we put it. Looking up the valley towards Brwynen and Bwlch-sych, snow still lay where the drifts had been.

Now I worked for Glyn Humphreys for about two and a half years, work which was new to me at that time. March was coming up to lambing time and Glyn kept good Welsh ewes at Llan. He never fed his ewes like they do today unless we had snow and then it was only feed out of a meal sack. Hay was loose in the barns so you pulled hay out by hand and into the sack. Thistles were the worse thing as I remember. I don't think they were so heavy stocked in the 1950s as we are today, so the sheep survived when we had no snow.

Lambing over, never troubled by foxes, plenty of rabbits for them to feed on. Next job was sorting the ewes with ram lambs from the ewes with ewe lambs; the barren had already gone to the hill. This job took most of the day, getting all the ewes and lambs together at the back of Llan and letting the ewes with ewe lambs run through between you and the dog. This was OK until near the end when a wrong sheep and lamb ran through, then the dog would fetch it back. Tempers were a little frayed before you finished the day. Ewes with ewe lambs to the hill, ram lambs kept down to grow and fatten. Next job, early June, gather the hill for tailing and ear marking.

First time I went up the mountain I thought it was a vast area. Glyn had gone to the far end on his Shire mare and when he got near home he let me ride so he could work his dogs better. It was just above the vicarage when Hugh Jones hit the mare on the bum with a stone. The mare shot off though the middle of the sheep, me hanging on for dear life until I got to the gate. Hugh and Glyn only laughed but I was not amused and told them so and I tell you what, I could hardly walk for two days. I walked around like a bow-legged jockey. It did hurt, I thought I was ruined for life.

Shearing time was the time I liked. All the neighbouring farmers came to shear about eight or so. I was taught to wrap the wool and put it into big wool sheets, twice the size we have today. The ewe lambs were sheared at Llan and they would have a shearing competition and Tommy, Bwlch-sych was the judge but I don't remember a prize.

Glyn taught me to plough with his Ford Standard, my first field to plough (after Glyn had done the headland and the first cop for me) was below the village shop and chapel. The next was a ten acre field on the Cefn road, it was wonderful up there. I remember Mrs Humphreys bringing up my lunch in a basket and laying a cloth on the grass, and while we had lunch I counted ten cuckoos flying towards Cefn, singing as they flew. The field was planted with stubble turnips to finish the lambs. A very good crop, I remember eating them when they were young, like eating apples.

The field below the shop was planted with oats and cut with the old Massey binder. When it was bought out of the barn, it would be covered in dust and feathers from the hens, but as long as the knotter was bright, the canvases and sails were clean it was OK.

Come thrashing time, it was great. Stan Clochnant with his tractor and Idris Jones (Jose, Ty-Cerrig's, brother) with the thrashing box. They were a partnership at thrashing time. Starting at Ty-Brith and working up the valley to Ty-Croes. Each farm killed a lamb at thrashing time and the dinners were wonderful stump mipe at each farm and trimmings. My job was to go to each farm to help with the thrashing.

Pitching sheaves onto the box was my job and killing rats when you got near the bottom of the bay. I soon found out why the farmers tied their trousers below the knee with string, because a rat went up my trouser leg and I was worried about my fishing tackle, I can tell you. On the back of the box was a reaping tackle which tied the straw in big sheaves until the big balers came into use.

Glyn grew also a little black oat, which was fed without thrashing. This was fed to the cows in the sheaves and it made the cows shine. Sadly Glyn sold up and went to farm at Red Castle Weston Rhyn until he retired.

It is now forty-eight years since we moved to Wales and a lot of changes have happened in those years, but I think Hirnant has gone back in time since the 50s.

Hirnant, in 1951, had a population of close on 100 people, now I should say it is perhaps twenty-five. In 51, church, chapel and school in use, a bus service every Wednesday, a shop and post office, a good road man in Bob Jenkins, a butcher at Pant-Cae-Hir, and Vagg's transport collecting milk churns from Llan milk stand each morning. I know the three children who went to the school had brothers or sisters to go to the school a year or two later, but the teacher Miss Griffiths, and Miss Jenkins the cook, both came to retirement age, so it was not worthwhile restarting fresh staff.

In Hirnant now, no shop or post office, no church, the chapel pulled down and made into a house in Pen-y-bont-fawr, the school now a bungalow, no farms selling milk, so things are going backwards instead of forwards, just the same as we are doing in Llanwddyn.

Mr Rowlands says about people going to church or chapel, (in numbers I mean), you read in the *Newsletter* about people who are ill in Llanwddyn, always people who go to church I notice, so, if people don't go to church you are never ill.

But getting back to my story — I called at Cefn early in the month and recalled a good story and told Mr and Mrs Humphreys about it. It was going back to 1952-53 before the mixi, I think my sister Margaret was working in the Lake Vyrnwy Hotel at the time. Well you see David Roberts, Cefn farmed land joined up with our land at Pen-y-Geuffordd, but Mr Roberts never set his land to a rabbit catcher, so all his rabbits used to eat our bit of grass at night time. (Not on!)

Now Mr Roberts was a deacon at the chapel in Hirnant, so on Sunday mornings Dad would get me six gills (female ferrets), put them in sand bags and Margaret and myself used to go into Mr Robert's wood overlooking Hirnant chapel and when Mr Roberts went into chapel our ferrets went into Mr Robert's rabbits' holes. After netting the holes we would wait and Margaret could hear better than me and she could hear the rabbits running underground and could tell me which net they were running to. I can tell you this, unless you put your foot over the hole when you were taking a rabbit out of the net you would lose another rabbit.

Remember a chapel service only lasted about an hour, so you would have to watch the time and make sure you had all your ferrets out of the warren before they came out of chapel. Perhaps you would have eight or ten rabbits in this time, so at 2/6 a pair it was quite good money in the 50s.

When Phillip came out of the RAF we became more mobile because Phil was quite keen on motorbikes and soon bought a 500 cc shaft driven Sunbeam with a box sidecar, and what he did was make ripples and a tailboard for the sidecar so we could take sows to the boar and goats to the billy, saving a lot of time and footwear. He also took little pigs to Welshpool or Oswestry markets. One time I remember him taking Dad to his brothers in Whitchurch and coming back home with Dad on the pillion and six bales of straw in the sidecar.

Phil did get a job with the old Liverpool Corporation as a wagoner, working with Glyn Jones and Maldwyn Lloyd. He did tell me one time about loading Jack Davies, Cammen Mawr with Christmas trees at Fronlas. After the load had gone, the gang wanted to go to the wet weather shed for dinner, so, Phil loading the sidecar with five men and one on the pillion set off for dinner and what happens, he caught the load of Christmas trees up round a corner towards the bottom of Glascwm and with the weight of his load he could not stop and ended up in the back of the load of trees and he lost half his personnel and was not very popular, but I think he had to buy a new headlight.

This is how we first started to come to Llanwddyn, on the Sunbeam and sidecar. On Friday nights before the centre bought its own projector we had films from Llanfyllin with the projector set up at the back of the hall and if I remember the hall was quite full and the first film we saw was 'The Last Days of Dolwen', which was very good. When we came out of the pictures we were strangers to the lads of Llanwddyn and being English took a while to make friends.

Raymond and Fredie Carpenter who lived at Gwreiddiau at the time and Raymond had a 350 cc Sunbeam. He would wait for Phil to start the bike for home and we would be above the wet weather shed when Raymond would go zooming past at speed.

F

When I was young I was bedridden for a number of years with polio but always wanted to get well and join in with other children and this is what I did. I always wanted to play football, to the extent of getting in trouble with the hospital with cracked and broken plaster casts on my leg. The hospital staff would patch me up or change the plaster cast and send me home on crutches with a ticking off. I think I would have made quite a good footballer because I was very keen at an early age even with my disability.

I always wanted to get into farming as my father came from a farming family, even though we lived in a council house. I always wanted to get on and live a good life. Mother was very strict and taught us good manners and not to smoke and drink. Mother used to tell me that her grandparents were mill owners in Bradford, but he drank all his money away, to the extent that her father never had a penny. This made her father become a big chapel man and a TT. This was the life my mother and sisters led; chapel three times a day on Sundays. This was the life I led until I got married, not drinking or smoking, not that June corrupted me but I will have a drink to be sociable, but it wouldn't worry me if all the pubs closed tomorrow. I remember going to the LVH when I was football secretary, selling raffle tickets and was told, you cannot sell raffle tickets here because you don't drink. My reply was that I was selling tickets for the village football team not my own pocket, nothing more was said.

When I first came to the village I didn't have many friends because I was TT so I became more interested in the pictures, football, whist drives and the youth club. Most of my local friends are boys and girls who used to come to attend the youth club etc. I can tell you how the spin off from these activities have given me great pleasure. We all know about the football in the 60s/70s. The fun we used to have when we had the pictures on Friday nights. The pleasure it gave me to look after the young at the youth club and badminton club, and it was nice to look after lads on trips when mothers used to say "You can go if Brian's going."

My oldest brother lives at Poulton-le-Fylde, about six miles out of Blackpool and I used to spend a week each year with them when I had my Royal Enfield. I would book a front seat at all the shows in Blackpool, they were 21/- a seat at that time.

Lonnie Donegan was at the Winter Gardens one year when he recorded 'My Old Man's a Dustman' and he nearly deafened me. I also went round the clubs but I will not tell you which and what clubs I went to, that would spoil the fun.

Maldwyn and Tommy Davies used to run a weekend bus to the lights at Blackpool and one or two nights were spent sleeping on the bus. One particular year, "You can go if Brian's going" and that was Colin, Berwyn, Gwyn O, Jones No 7 and Peter Jones No 5. I suppose we went into Blackpool, round the town and pleasure beach, but one place we did go was Madam Tussaud's. You paid and went through a revolving door, but poor old Colin paid and went round the revolving door and out into the street again. You could see him on TV inside waiting for us outside.

"Where are we going now Bri?" I was asked.

"Well I know a little club" I said "we could go there first." (I had booked seats to see Ken Dodd at the Winter Gardens later.) Well we went to this club towards the South Pier and I laughed more at these lads than I did at the show, say no more! Time was getting on and I didn't want to miss Ken Dodd so we ran all across Blackpool dodging cars and buses, but we did get there on time and enjoyed the show. I tell you what! Berwyn went to sleep and never saw the show.

We had a bus to London to watch Spurs v Leicester when Gordon Banks was in goal for Leicester. To the match we went,

"You can go if Brian's going." Neil and Peter Jones were with me and I think Spurs won 1 - 0. The trouble was, John Derrick, after the match, said shall we get on the Tube and go to Soho. Neil and Peter were too young to go, so Brian stayed with them, but it seemed hours before the party arrived back on the bus, some worse for drink and I remember Jack Carsley telling me on the Monday morning, all about Soho. Ho-Ho-Ho.

After starting to work for the Liverpool Corporation in January 1957, my first job was to sort, stack and load rails with the late Tom Watkins. This took us up to June 1957 when we started to work in the late Emyr Lloyd's gang, which was a big gang of around twenty plus. We were transported in Peter Barrett's lorry, which was full. My first job with the gang was to be saw-brashing in the Brynadda area, which was a vast area of Sitka, Norway, Douglas and Larch which took all of the summer of 1957. This was where I first met Ray Jandrell and we have been friends ever since. This was a mixed gang of men, from school leavers up to men nearing pension age and you can understand the gang being in two parts.

An hour for dinner in the early days, and dinner would be taken in about ten mins, to leave us to play cricket for forty-five mins with a cricket bat made by Ray and the stumps were the gate post at the bottom of Brynadda Road. Our cricket team would be Ray, Don Bisset, Henry, Mervyn, George Edwards, Ken Lloyd, Len Davies and myself.

We moved at the end of summer to Hafod, same job but much wetter weather. Our dinner cabin was the old Hafod farmhouse with an old-fashioned open fire, and when we went for dinner each day we were supposed to take a dead rail or some form of fire wood to save Harry Probert's wood, but it was wet that winter. When we finished brashing the area and moved to Cedig we had burnt all Harry's wood.

The cricket season had now turned to football season and outside Hafod house was a patch of grass to play football but we didn't have a ball. Ray was going to see his parents in Oswestry so we all chipped in to buy a ball from Woolies for twenty-one shillings. A cheap ball but it lasted quite a while. Ray would take it home to Eunant at night to stitch up the panels, and then it burst so we filled it with old hay and kicked hell out of it. On wet days it was wrestling in the old hay barn until we found out it contained fleas and that was the end to wrestling.

As you know my home town was Whitchurch and on August bank holiday a good show was held on that day. I asked Ray whether he would like to go to the show with me on the pillion of my Royal Enfield and he said yes. So I ended up waiting for him by Dafarn shop at 8.30 a.m. but he never turned up because I had told him 9.30. Well we had a violent thunderstorm after the show, and on the way home the road was lit up by lightning all the way. So it was just as well he missed me because I was soaked even though I had a Black Prince motorbike suit on.

The following year we did go on my brother's 750cc twin Royal Enfield. We stopped at Ellesmere for a break and Ray said his leg was burning. We inspected it to find out that I had overfilled the battery and the acid had boiled up and run onto Ray's trouser leg. By the end of the day Ray's trouser leg was all holes. He pulled up his sock and the top came off, his sole came off his shoe and for some reason Margaret was not very pleased when Ray arrived home. But we did get to the show and enjoyed it.

The following year I hired Tommy Davies to take a bus to the show and what fun we had with Trevor Hill and Jack Carsley. Ray and I remembered the show from the year before and went round the show with them. We went to a tent to watch a stripper, nothing rude of course, she worked with feather fans. Trevor and Jack were up front and I can see Trevor now, trying to blow the feathers away. Such a laugh and Jack going "Ho, Ho, Ho." After that it was the wrestling booth and boxing. A lad who I went to school with took on the son of the man who owned the booth and if you could last three rounds you earned £5. He lasted three rounds but had a pasting. We all had a good day but sadly there is no longer a Whitchurch Show and Carnival.

For most of the way home Ray sang "Lloyd George Knew my Father, Father Knew Lloyd George" and if you know Ray's version, we were glad to see Llanwddyn again.

When I first started to work at Llan Farm, Hirnant, I suppose I was lucky to get a job so quickly, even in 1951, in such a small village as Hirnant. We had only been living at Pen-y-Geufford about a week, when I was offered a job at Llan by Glyn Humphreys.

When we left Whitchurch in 1951 I had had just one job after leaving school in 1949 and combined harvesters and pick-up balers were being used then. Moving to Wales was like turning the clock back twenty years. Each farm in Hirnant had one or two teams of Shire horses, the grass mower and binder were still worked by a team. The old Ford Standard was the main tractor used.

There was side-land set with corn which had been ploughed and worked by horses. This was cut by scythe and bound by hand, something I had never seen done before, let alone have to do it.

During my days with the Liverpool Corporation, in the 50s and 60s we had to do fire patrol at weekends in the summer months. This entailed seven men each day, four round the lake on bicycles, one down the Hirnant road, one in Conwy Valley as far as Rhydyryddan, which could be on motorcycle and one on the Bala Road beyond Fedw Ddu on motorcycle. I used to get Bala Road or Conwy Valley on my motorcycle. The job was to stop people lighting fires, paddling in the water or dogs swimming in the water. But people never do these things today, so I suppose that is why fire patrol has stopped! You may laugh!

In 1959 when the lake went very low for the first time, we talk about traffic today, but then you could not move round the lake for visitors, it came out on TV that the church spire was visible at Lake Vyrnwy, that was all that was needed. I was on patrol round the lake one Sunday when there was a traffic jam between Llechwedd Ddu and Hafod and I passed the late Ivor Vaughan sitting in his car and he said "Where do I send the bill to Dawson, I've been sitting here for over an hour." A car's half shaft had broken and blocked the road.

Things seemed different then, visitors brought picnics with them and sat outside their cars to eat them. When on patrol on Sundays, cars would be bumper to bumper from Ty-Mawr fields all the way to Allforgan, but today most visitors seem to go to the workshops and never go round the lake at all.

A few tricks played by men at work which stand out in my mind — Fred Wilcock second man for George Jones on D6. Len Davies brought Fred a swiss roll from Mrs Hill, but what George had told Len to do was stick a six inch nail down the middle of the swiss roll, cover the cream over the nail and give it to Fred. Now George knew Fred would share it with him at dinner time. So, at dinner time, out comes the swiss roll. "Piece of swiss roll George?"

"OK Fred." Fred gets out his penknife to cut the roll but all you could hear was, "You bugger, you bugger."

Len on his way to work, dug up some bluebell bulbs, washed them, tied them with a piece of string and brought them to the wet weather shed and offered them to Jose Ty-Cerrig as spring onions. Jose accepted them and offered tomatoes in return, but Len had to tell him and Jose only laughed.

When you were in a big gang with men and lads, you always got the element of young or the older men, which they enjoyed. Men like Percy Hughes, Gommer Isaac, H. C. Johnson, etc., loved to be tormented. Percy, planting Christmas trees on the lakeside. Mervyn tying his bicycle chain to its frame with a piece of wire. Going home Percy jumps on his bicycle, starts to pedal and falls off. Mervyn says, "What's the matter Percy?" But I cannot print what he replied!

Saw bashing with Emyr's gang by Bwlch-sych mountain, and

finding a tin of sheep marking raddle (red). Percy always took a terrier to work and she was a friendly little girl, talk to anyone, so Gary Hill gets the raddle and puts some on the terrier. Being a wet day, it ended red all over. Nobody had done it at all, of course. Percy was not amused about his red dog so he reported us to Alf Veoney, the forester. By morning the dog was back to normal but we still got told off by the forester. Percy was now back to normal, ready for more tricks to be played on him.

Harry Hughes on the D4, always had an old kettle to boil for dinner, but one day he must have left the lid off the kettle. Jack 19 fills his kettle to boil and when Harry takes the lid off to brew his tea, a frog must have been in the kettle and had been boiled alive. I think he had tea off the gang this day.

Waiting in the bus shelter by the office one summer morning in 1960 with Jack, waiting for a lorry to pick us up to load rails, across the dam came a strange vehicle. What it turned out to be was just a chassis and cab of an old Liverpool bus with the driver looking like Biggles sitting in the cab, no doors or windscreen, flying helmet, goggles, gauntlet gloves and a big heavy overcoat, it still must have been cold driving all the way from Liverpool.

Shoreys' workshop was by where the new toilets are now and the strange vehicle was for Harold and John to make a low-loader to move the D4 and D6 from place to place. When the low-loader was finished, driver of the D6, George, had the job of driving this monster. When driving George always had someone to help him because it was so heavy to steer. It had a pre-select gear box and a big Gardner engine. It went quite well for a while but I think the D6 was too heavy and broke the low-loader's back and it finished its day in the wet weather shed where it stood for about six years before it went for scrap. It served a good purpose in the shed for keeping sheep netting on and as a windbreak when the shed doors were open.

I think it must have been in the early 70s before we had electric and water laid on for toilets and drinking water. By now Jack Tan-y-Ffordd had retired and Peter Barrett and Jim Hale came to help at the shed. Peter on the peeler and Jim on the pickling tanks.

After getting married, Ron Stokes, assistant forester at the time, wanted a small gang to produce rails, stakes, and Liverpool poles on the lakeside near Llechwedd-Du, so Henry, John Factory and myself were picked to do this job which lasted for about two years or more. We had to fall a big area above and below Bryngwyn Road all the way to Llechwedd-Du. Falling, brashing out and stacking. Gwil had the job of tushing out with Doug Buttery's horse. One morning just after we started the job. Gwil's horse decided he had had enough so instead of stopping at the dump the horse decided to go home and off he went past the office with a tush of rails behind him. I think Gwil found the horse and rails by Top Shop.

After we had been going for a while, we had the McConnell saw sent up and the rails were cut into Liverpool poles, stakes and hedge stakes, all pointed and stacked all ready for loading. No 'Hiabs' for loading at this time. I remember we loaded John Ransford with hedge stakes. It took nearly all morning to load 3,000 stakes. Moving from place to place, this job was summer and winter and I think in the winter of 1970 we didn't have any snow and hardly any frost.

Things were getting a bit mod at the shed, so I left Henry and John. Roger had joined them by now and I was back with Jack. A new electric pickling plant was installed. The stakes were put in cradles and lifted in and out with the front end loader, the creosote was pumped by electric from tank to tank.

Peter and Jim had retired by now and Sam Hill was at the shed. I had Sam's Fergie and the main job was going around with the piss-pot urea. Mr Westlake was now head forester and Gordon Griffiths was second in command. A great man Gordon, a good village man as was his wife. Gordon was with us for quite a number of years, taking over after Mr Kelly had died and then Mr Westlake died.

I think Gordon and David Rowlands could have run the estate very well but it was not to be. With the new creosote tanks in full swing producing thousands of stakes and also selling them very well, by now Jack had retired and Henry came to me at the shed, of course we were on piece work by now on everything we did. We were together for a number of years and by now we were making 100 stakes per hour, pickling seven days per week. Like they say, all good things come to an end, Sam had by now retired and Henry and myself were left alone at the shed. Mr Dugglesby came to me and said the shed work was coming to an end as it was not paying; we were gob-smacked because I can tell you this, if the shed work did not pay, nothing paid, look what they are doing today, selling timber and buying stakes from ETC.

My last two years were spent with the Fergie and working alongside the gangs which were left by now, it was not the same and when the time came for me to be able to take early retirement I took it with open arms in 1985.

In conclusion to this story I would like to thank the many men I had worked with in those twenty-eight years, for making life and work worthwhile.

*Mervyn, the author and Ray at Hafod.*
*Ray passed away in 2004, aged sixty-seven years.*

In the summer of 1960 the Liverpool Corporation purchased a large number of concrete sleepers weighing 2½ cwt each for a number of uses but mainly for culverts on forestry roads. The sleepers were bought from the old Kinerley army camp and were all lifted and in piles. The farm tractor with Evan Tom I think, loaded the forestry lorries and were tipped all around the wet weather shed. Jack Tany-Ffordd and Jackie Tanycaer along with Jack and myself had the job of stacking these sleepers, it was a heavy job and you had to watch your fingers.

Now Jackie, the devil he was. I was watching him one day and what he was doing (remember it was very hot), he was stunning a fly on the back of his hand and putting the fly gently on a spider's web and watching the spider come down the web and catch the fly and devour it.

Jackie was also a great auctioneer. On a wet day in the shed, if he was in the right mood, he would sell anything in the shed and the rest of the gang were the buyers.

One of the things Jack liked to do when we were on the lakeside, was going down to the office once a week with his jerry can on his bicycle handlebars, for petrol for the saw. This would take all morning. He would chat with Felex in the stores, mainly about dominoes (Felex played a lot in the hotel with Jack), and of course football. Felex was a keen Llanwddyn supporter. He would have a chat with anyone around the office. I remember him telling me about meeting Mr Howard on the lakeside, with a bag of logs on his handlebars. Mr Howard stops Jack and asks "What have you got in your bag Jack?"

Quick as a flash, Jack replies "Tatters Sir." Mr Howard knew quite well what Jack had in his sack.

The stakes we made and pickled were for the estate use only until we moved to the shed. Joe Waen would collect 500 and take them down to the yard for stock and the tractors would collect to take stakes directly to the job. We also split a lot of rails for the pipe track down Oswestry way.

Mr Kelly came one morning and quite out of the blue told Jack and myself to report to the wet weather shed next morning (1961). This was a big shock to Jack because it had been his base near home for about twenty years. I missed the old pickler as well because it was so quiet and peaceful, but of course it was nearer home for me.

The wet weather shed as I understand, was built in the early 50s with money from the sale of Christmas trees the previous year. Jones the Coed was the forester then and he had the shed built. Just a big, high, basic shed, cold, damp, no electric, no toilets, just two pot-bellied stoves either side of the building. When you lit the stoves on a damp morning, the shed filled with smoke until they warmed up. Outside and upside down were two big iron tanks which had been standing for around ten years, which were to be our pickling tanks for the future. The old pickler was dismantled, Jack and I had it for firewood. The two pickling tanks and the saw were taken to the shed and that was the end of the old pickler. What remains is a horse chestnut tree at the entrance to the place which holds happy times to me and I am sure Jack loved it too.

Trevor's gang erected two old pickling tanks, first the old buoy out of the lake was erected on concrete sleepers and worked a treat. The old rocket was as good as ever but the other two big tanks only stood for a further two years (again with Trevor's gang, they were erected with much skill I must add), because they worked flat out even at weekends, latterly from 1965-1980, making thousands of stakes and posts. On fine days Sam would take the old Liner saw outside for Jack and myself to work, wet times inside the shed. Now if we were out and it came to rain, Jack would stop the saw and cover her with a tarpaulin made for the job. Now remember — No electricity! No toilet! — one hell of a long way to walk!

We did get used to the shed. Jack used to arrive about 8.30 a.m. after stopping by Daffern with the gangs and foresters. I progressed to a little Ford van, after moving to Brwynen in 1964, now it was my turn to take a little fire wood home. In the days I started work in 1957 until I married in 1970, Jack and I were always on day work, not very good money but you can manage when you are single.

I suppose we had been at the shed two years when two new diesel McConnell saws and a new Cundey Peeler arrived. Jack and I used both the new saws for a while and peeled outside when it was dry.

Jack Tany-Ffordd came to the shed to work as his leg was not too good and he was also sixty. Jackie went into Trevor's gang. Jack was very good, he kept the two fires going, boiled the cans and hand peeled the stakes, stacking them round the fires. By now I had passed my driving test in the van and it came about two weeks later that John Wiblyn the second in charge had a new van but had not passed his driving test. So I was asked to travel around with him as the experienced driver, this I did for around eighteen months, collecting him each morning, taking him to Daffern and then to the office. I would then go to the shed, help Jack if I was needed. Kelly would bring John down from the office to collect me as I had the van. I would have to go round the gangs with him on pay days because this was how we were paid then, by the forester taking pay out to all the workers.

I went with John on his driving tests (three times) to Machynelleth, passing on the third attempt. Sadly John died after leaving Llanwddyn. He left a wife and three young children.

After falling a sycamore tree for sink draining boards and cutting it into lengths with a cross cut saw, Jack said come to the house for a cup of tea but I declined because he had a sheepdog which was funny so I asked him to bring a cup down. I was sorry after because I had never met Jack's mum, I think she was in her eighties, and she died a few months after. While Jack was fetching the tea I sat on the tree and looked at this big house below a forest of Jap larch and thought what a lovely place to live, little was I to know that eleven years later I would be married and living there myself, but that is another story.

Jack talked of his school days quite a lot, how he used to walk to school in Glanrafen, about one and a half miles, and how he had a stick and hoop to bowl along. He said it used to shine like a sixpence and get him to school quicker. Fifty or more children went to his school, from four years to school leavers, all under one roof with three teachers.

Jack Willy talked of days as a lad working at Bryngwyn for two old ladies. A lot of Welsh ponies ran that side of the valley before it was planted. Jack talked of Thomas Vaughan a blind man who lived at Ty-Vaughan, a smallholding beyond Bryngwyn. He used to walk to the hotel quite often with a stick and when he got to the lakeside he would tap the railing with his stick. Courting couples thought the Devil was coming when they heard the tapping on the lakeside fence.

Jack never liked the gang coming to the pickler on wet-time because we could not 'Saw' for safety reasons plus you could not get near the fire if Emyr's gang came, about fifteen to twenty men. Young lads pretended to take Jack's fire wood to get him naggy. Then the gang would settle down to a game of 'tip-it' and it would go quiet. Tip-it was a game played with two teams of three. One team would be 'in', with a little stone in the hand of one player. Up would come the hands and the other team would have to tip the hand with the stone in. It was the first to ten to win, it was quite a good game really.

I travelled to work on a motorcycle in the 50-60s not so many cars then but quite a lot of motorcycles. I first had a 350cc Royal Enfield then a BSA 500cc Trails Bike and finished with an Aerial Leader 250cc, quite a nice motorbike. George and Betty bought it off me and had it quite a while.

Now around this time we had quite a change in foresters. Alf Veini moved on, quite a character, Alf. A lot of the men called him 'Trekle Feet' because he travelled around the gangs on a BSA Bantam or Bantam Major motorbike. (No posh Land Rovers then.) A tall man, with a big moustache and wore glasses. He wore a helmet and a big long black raincoat and wellies. When he talked to you he pattered from one foot to the other just as though his feet were stuck in treacle, hence the name "Trekle Feet". Head forester John Lomas retired. Mr Kelly was then made up to head forester. Then came John Widlyn in place of Alf, what a lovely man. Gordon Griffiths was the only forester who came up to his standard to work for.

Jack kept two cows at Llechwedd-Du while I worked with him but he never seemed to have any calves. I asked him one day why and he told me it was very awkward with AI, getting to the phone. I think he used to walk them to Dai Dairy's in the past. He had difficulty making hay because of the notorious Llechwedd-Du gnats plus Jack used to get a little thirsty in the summer time. He sold his two old cows to Watkin Richards, a dealer at that time. I then grazed the ground with four young cattle, a bit of beer money for Jack.

The job I loved was collecting the creosote barrels from Llanfyllin Station. Joe Waen would collect Jack, myself and twelve empty forty-five gallon drums from the pickler, go to Llanfyllin Station collect twelve full ones and Jack would always insist on having dinner at the New Inn, a change from having a cup of tea I suppose. I remember being there one time when George Parkes drove ten Shire horses through Llanfyllin and loaded them at the station into trucks.

We were very busy at Liverpool Show time. Trevor Hill would be making rustic work down at the wet weather shed. Sam or Peter would be up and down all day with orders for Trevor, "Cut me this," "Cut me that," it was a job which lasted for about a month. Then Trevor's gang would go to Liverpool for two weeks to erect the forestry stand. Jack used to go himself years before and it sounded as if it was as good as a holiday.

The time had come when I was getting involved with the football club and to raise money for the club I reared quite a lot of cockerels in battery cages and used to get them to around 10lb body weight each. In the winter months take one to work, pluck it on a Thursday dinner time, take it home, Dad would dress it, take it to work and the hotel would raffle it at 3d a ticket, draw the ticket at the home or away game and give the profit over the value of the chicken to the club.

One time the Rev Hopkin Evans arrived at the pickler on horseback. Jack Groes had just castrated the horses and told Hopkin to take the horses for exercise. Hopkin called quite often for a few stakes, what a character for a vicar.

The time came when the contractors and our own gangs had to paint all the tree stumps after falling, a waste of time but had to be done just the same. First they started to paint them with creosote, and now use urea. This as I understand is why we had to move to the wet weather shed, because traces of creosote had been found in water from the lake. This was quite understandable because all barrels of creosote were placed over a drain to make it easy to fill a gallon tin from the barrel tap; where do all the drains end up? in the lake.

Sam Hill and I carried the piss-pot as it was called with Sam on the old Ford Standard tractor and later with 35 Fergie. I also did it for years until I retired, now it is done with a nice warm Land Rover.

I want to tell you about perhaps the happiest years of my life.

In January 1957 I started work for the then Liverpool Corporation on the Forestry Department, starting work first day with the late Tom Watkins, Ty-Fedw, who was also on his first day.

I would like to list the men and young men who worked on the Forestry Department in 1957.

Trevor Hill's gang — Trevor Hill himself, George and Joe Morris, Wil Williams, Tom Carsley, Brian Roberts, Ted Furber, H. C. Johnson, George Evans, Joss Jones, Jackie Evans, Jack Tanffordd, and Don Humphreys.

Emyr Lloyd's gang — Emyr himself, Tom Watkins, myself, Henry Jones, Ray Jandrell, Gomer Isaac, I. Lloyd, Jack Lloyd, Albert Owen, Ken Lloyd, Don Bissett, Harry Hughes Pen-y-bont-fawr.

Road gang — Ron and Sim Carpenter, George Edwards, Len Davies, Sam Hill, Jack 19, George Jones, Harry Hughes, Fred Wilcox, Elwyn Roberts, Dai Owen, Peter Barrett and Maldwyn Davies.

'Old pickler keepers' — Jack Carsley, Sam Probert, Joe Millington, Percy Hughes, Walter Carpenter.

'Blue-eyed gang markers' — Jim Hughes, J. D. Hughes, Merfyn Davies.

'Foresters Waggoners' — Alf Veonce, Ses Kelly, John Lomas, also Maldwyn Lloyd and Glyn Jones.

Remember this was before power saws, double drum winches, etc.; axes and 'bushmen' were the tools of the day. The first job we had was loading rails, Tom Watkins and I. This lasted from January to the end of June 1957.

The job entailed sorting out rails into different sizes, stacking in sizes and loading whatever size the farmer wanted. They were at Glasgwm and Fedw Dda on the Bala road. The rails had come from the trees that Trevor's gang had felled from October to December the previous year for Christmas trees; falling the trees with a six or seven pound axe and pulling the Christmas tree to the nearest ride.

After Christmas, the 'gang' would go back and brash out the trees with a two and a half pound axe and then stack them in the ride ready for Maldwyn and Glyn to pull them out with horses or Harry and Jack 19 to pull them out with a D4 cat (hence Brian and Tom loading and sorting rails).

Pay was every fortnight when you had to meet the 'pay clerk' on the nearest main road. The pay clerk came from Liverpool and stayed at the hotel. We also worked on Saturday mornings until the 60s. Only one forest road had been completed by this time, and you had quite a long way to walk before you got to your job. I have seen the time when it has been 9.30-10 a.m. before getting started.

Starting work with Emyr's gang as a member proper was in 1957; saw brashing was the main job in those days which entailed pruning every tree to six feet six inches so that you could walk under the forest at any time or place. This was the first time I had met Ray Jandrell and we have been friends ever since.

We had one hour for dinner at this time, so you can tell this was too long to sit about after dinner; so we used to play cricket using the gate post at Brynadda for the wicket. I can see Don Bissett now bowling his leg breaker and smoking a fag at the same time.

Each gang had a 'can lad'. This was usually the youngest lad in the gang. I think ours was Henry at that time. His job was to get a good fire going for around 11 a.m., fill the cans with water from the nearest stream and have all cans boiling by twelve or thereabouts. The best laugh I had with a 'can lad' was with Ronnie Hill by Cyneddwen on the lakeside. We were cutting Christmas trees, Mr Kelly came around with Emyr looking at trees. Ron had a length of pipe and borrowed a little petrol out of Mr Kelly's van. Now the funny part about this was, Ron had built a nice fire, filled the cans, put them round the fire and lit it. But as he lit it he caused a small explosion which blew all the cans over and split the water, it was a real laugh.

Saw brashing at Hafod — winter 58. We were carried by lorry now, but had to walk from the lakeside to the job. But if it was wet you had to walk to Hafod House. This was our depot and once it rained for three days and all we did was walk to Hafod and back.

We were working at Hafod when the Manchester United players were killed in that terrible plane crash (Munich). We all pooled in to buy a football from Woolies for twenty-one shillings and played football at dinner time. The ball went like lead when it got wet. Ray was always stitching up the ball and when the bladder finally burst we filled it with hay and carried on.

Working in Cedig was very interesting because it had never been explored for many years and was a vast area. At one time we had to fell trees across the river to make bridges. I think we made three bridges, the last one by the fence at Fotty. Now this was long and very spongy. We had a few in the gang that played tricks; Merfyn was the main culprit and we would cross the bridge, and when Percy Hughes was half way across, start to bounce up and down and make Percy hold on for dear life, or catch him and dangle him over the river until he shouted for dear life.

On the other side of the valley beyond Ty-Ucha we started to brash and fell the road lines, and this is where the power saw first came into action. Tom Carsley and George Edwards had the saw and felled the beech, and the rest of the gang felled the small trees.

The chain never stopped running on the chainsaw, but when you started it, it kicked like hell. I can see Tom Carsley chucking the chainsaw down the woods with a few swear words to follow.

In the November of 1958, I was cutting Christmas trees on the lakeside with Emyr's gang , when our forester came to me and said, "Brian I want you to start work with Jack Carsley at the Old Pickler on Monday."

And I worked with Jack for nearly sixteen years, the best mate a man could ever wish to work with.

The Old Pickler was situated about half a mile from Llechwedd-Du, right by the big horse chestnut tree on the lakeside. Sam Probert had retired so Jack needed a new mate, and he talked about football, horse racing and the hotel, so that suited me OK.

Jack had lived at Llechwedd-Du with his mother, Tom, Sarah, Michael, Evelyn, Kath and Jack Williams. Jack had moved to Llechwedd-Du from Glanrafon when he was three years old; the oldest of five children. His father had died in 1947. Jack's father was the first forester at Lake Vyrnwy and it was he who had all the lovely big trees planted that are around the lake today. Jack's mother was born in the old village at a house called Minffrwd and she was a pastry cook at the Lake Vyrnwy Hotel when it was first built.

Jack's father was born at Ellesmere, and after leaving school he went as a gardener to the Buckley Arms in Dinas Mawddwy. After a few years a forester was needed at Lake Vyrnwy, this was well before the Forestry Commission came into being. This was a bit of history about the great John Halmer Carsley.

Jim Hale (who was a logger at Llechwedd-Du after moving from Liverpool before the war), once said to me "If a person needed a place in heaven it would be Jack." He was a gentle giant (six feet two inches).

The Old Pickler was built just after the war, by I think, Dai Morris Revel. It was built with air pipes from Cowney Tunnel. It was made for men to work in on wet time and for the nursery work for nearby. My job with Jack was second man on the saw bench, which was an old petrol Liner. Making stakes and splitting rails for the estate was our main job, also creosoting the stakes after they had been peeled and dried. We had two pickle tanks, one held over 100 stakes, the other twenty longer stakes. One was an old buoy from off the lake (from during the war), with the rivets cut off the top to make a tank. This was put in the ground with a fire underneath and stakes were pickled twice a week.

The other old tank, I think must have come out of the Ark, it was like an open train with a chimney at one end. (I think it is still on the side of Celyn Road.)

Sometimes we had to cut fire wood for the bosses. Jack and myself would go out and fell a number of beech trees with crosscut saw or bushmans and branch the trees with an axe. Sam Hill would come with the old Ford Standard tractor and trailer and load the beech to be taken to the pickler to be cut into logs and delivered to whoever needed them.

Now the making of the stakes was quite an art. Jack would push the stake length so far through the saw and I would pull them the rest of the way. Jack would then point them. As he pointed, I would take the chips off the bench and chuck them into two piles, dry ones and wet ones. Now somehow Jack knew how many stakes to cut to fill two sacks of logs, one to take home at dinner time and one at night, but we always seemed to cut more to make sure we had a couple of bags for the weekend. The wet chips were used on the pickler fires.

Our fire for boiling the cans was an old forty-five gallon drum with the front cut out and a chimney on top out through the roof. We lit the fires with what Jack called 'Burr-goo', this was made in an old pan with sawdust and creosote made like porridge, it burnt for hours. Our seats were shearing benches and stakes were stacked all round the fire at a safe distance. Jack never liked to leave the pickler to work elsewhere, even though Mr Kelly, our forester was married to Jack's sister Edie May, I don't think we had any favours from him!

Sometimes we had to go out loading rails or Liverpool poles, which were tree stakes made for Liverpool Council for new housing estates. This was Jack Tanyrffordd and Jackie Tan-y-caeau's job at that time. Falling rails and cutting them into ten, twelve and fifteen feet lengths and pointing them. A chap called Alex Duckworth would bring a load of second-hand iron pipes from Liverpool for forestry road culverts, pick Jack and myself up and unload the pipes at the wet weather shed and take a load of poles back to Liverpool. The Liverpool poles job got quite big and lasted for about ten years. Trevor's gang did the job, then lastly Henry, John Factory and myself had the saw out in the woods and made thousands of them. Maldwyn Davies and Peter Barrett were always taking poles to Liverpool.

During the summer holidays, Sarah, Evelyn and Kath would call at the pickler for a chat and a rest on the way to the Top Shop, or to meet the bus on a Wednesday. John Williams, or Jack Willy as he was called, would be on his way to Top Shop to do odd jobs for the Owens. Jack was in his late seventies or early eighties.

One day Jack was there when Kelly called, he wanted Jack and myself to fell a sycamore tree for Stef at the saw mill to cut into draining boards for the estate. A dead tree if possible, ready seasoned. Jack Willy pipes up, "I know where there's a good dead sycamore" and pointed out to Kelly a lone dead tree the other side of the lake below Nant-y-coedwr mountain. It appears Jack Willy was born there in a shepherd's cottage eighty years ago at a cottage called Dwrffordd but he told Kelly and laughed. "It's no good, it's full of nails. We used to knock horse nails into it when we were kids."

Kelly told Jack, "You want your arse kicking." But we did get a tree near to Llechwedd-Du and fell it with a crosscut saw and cut it into six foot lengths. Jack was not short of fire wood for a while!

Our village is getting very untidy and unkempt. I blame the council and forestry for the unkempt verges (council) and overgrown scrub and coppice above the grass verges and forestry roads (forestry). They do try but leave things far too late before tackling the problem. Look at the grass cutting round the lake. They leave it until the lovely holidaymakers have finished and then decide to cut the grass. Nearly October this year and then it is dragged off, not cut off, what a mess!

Then we have a hedge cutter round to cut the willow coppice etc., but it is not cut off, it is ripped off. At the back of Brwynen it was even cutting snow. I think everywhere looks a mess as do a lot of people. I think most of it is due to the lack of a resident forester, living and taking an interest in the estate and of course lack of manpower.

When I first started on the forestry, all the coppice and shrub was cut between the road and forestry, this was a job every year. Round the lakeside they even screefed a metre between forest and road. When I was in the gang saw brashing, you had to cut all the hardwood as going up the rows of trees, brashing this was, all part of a day's work — look at it now.

What is the first thing you notice when you come into the village. An untidy clear. Fall above the shop. Pounds of timber left to rot and a danger to the village. Get a hard frost and the tree stumps left behind will start to roll, and Cled will need another new fence. How many people know a lovely river or brook that runs alongside the road between Ty-Cerrig and the bottom of Glascwim Bank, now willow has taken over where a fence used to be.

What I can't understand is this, we are now in the year 2000 and supposed to be advanced with a handful of men, but in the 20s, 30s and 40s around 100 men were employed. Where did the money come from to pay 100 men when the Severn Trent begrudge paying what we have left. All the Severn Trent want is profit, that's all there is to it.

The lakeside is a mess, let's face it. They are making a good job of painting the lakeside fences, what is left that is, but I think it would be tidy if say a gang of three men, one in charge, cut all the hardwood scrub and any dead trees, sell the fire wood and any big conifers go for mill timber and plant Christmas trees where possible like they used to do. It would find work and keep the lakeside tidy.

In the 1956-57 season the village football team was first formed as a club in the name of Llanwddyn AFC.

Committee Members, 1956:
>Mr John Lomas, 17 Abertridwr
>Mr William Bull, 20 Abertridwr
>Mr Tom Hampton, 19 Abertridwr
>Mr Don Bissett, Frongoch
>Mr William Jones, 10 Abertridwr
>Mr John Thomas, Eagle's Nest
>Mr Eddie Thomas, Vyrnwy Stores
>Mr Emlyn Jones, School House
>Chairman: Mr J. Lomas
>Secretary: Mr D. Bissett
>Treasurer: Mr W. Bull

The meeting, held on Thursday 11-10-56, was the first club meeting ever. With money in hand of 17s 1d it was decided to ask every person wishing to be a club member to pay a senior membership of 2s 6d and junior membership 1s. Ways and means of raising money were discussed, and a whist drive, dance and raffle were proposed. Mr John Thomas, Eagle's Nest, then said his father was willing to support the club with money if it showed signs of success. The whist drive prizes were set at £4 and £1 for the raffle donated by Mr Bill Thomas.

The names of paid up members for the 1956-57 season:

T. Hampton, 19 Abertridwr
Ray Jandrell, Eunant
D. M. Davies, Ty-Llwyd
Henry Jones, Abermarchnant
Don Bissett, Frongoch
Elwyn William, Cefn Llwyni
Eddie Thomas, Vyrnwy Stores
Emlyn Jones, School House
R. E. Roberts, 1 Glanrafon
Allan Weaver, Grwn Oer
Roy Kelly, Tan-y-Bryn
David Rowlands, Fron Heulog
Brian Dawson, Pen-y-Geuffordd
Mr J. Thomas, 31 Abertridwr
Mr W. Bull, 20 Abertridwr
Arthur Lloyd, 15 Abertridwr
Ted Furber, Gwreiddiau
T. Thomas, Groes
Gary Hill, Bodlondeb
Tec Hughes, 10 Abertridwr
C. Vaughan, Factory
John Thomas, Eagle's Nest
Mr J. Lomas, 17 Abertridwr
Alf Vionie, Nantllachar
John Propert, Bryngwyn
Ken Lloyd, 14 Abertridwr
William Jones, 10 Abertridwr
I. E. Lloyd, 15 Abertridwr
Mr C. Kelly, Tanybryn
E. T. Lloyd, 2 Abertridwr
Mrs Isaacs, Fron Las.

The Llanwddyn AFC played in the old Oswestry District League, playing the first game in September 1959. This was the first competitive football in Llanwddyn as regards to league football.

The teams in the league were: Llanwddyn, Llanrhaeadr, Chirk Res, St Martins and Kinnerley.

Each team played four matches instead of two so that the teams could have a few more matches. As I remember Chirk was the top team at that time, but Llanwddyn did quite well considering the catchment area for signing players.

One match that I remember well was at Chirk; we were having a bit of stick when Tec Hughes in goal got a kick on the thumb and had to be taken to Chirk Hospital to have it treated. We then went on to lose 11-0. Tec came out of hospital onto the bus all bandaged up, and we still sang on the way home: "Are we down hearted, no dear no, Sometimes we win, sometimes we lose, Are we down hearted, no dear no". But in those days we didn't win any!

This league only lasted one season as St Martins dropped out, and the teams that were left couldn't really make a league.

In 1961-62 Llanwddyn entered the Mont Amateur League and have been with them ever since, unlike some of the other local teams! Over thirty years Amateur League.

In the 1961-62 season seventeen teams in one league only were entered, giving the clubs thirty-two league matches as well as the Mont Challenge Cup. The first few seasons were very hard with some very good teams in the league in those days, namely Trewern, Forden, etc.

The first win in the Amateur League to shock everybody was at home to Forden. I think the score was 2-1, but Forden did protest, saying the pitch was too small, but we still kept the points.

Llanwddyn did get some thrashings in the early seasons but they still carried on, sometimes starting with nine or ten players. One match we went to in Carno we had eight players on the bus; a wet day, and supporters in wellies. David Rowlands, captain on the day, said "Come on lads. Come and make a team," so Peter Jones, No 7, Berwyn and myself played in wellies. Now you might think that funny, but that was the start of big Peter playing. We were losing 11-0 but Ray has to go and challenge the Carno keeper — keeper clears the ball, ball hits Ray on the backside and rebounds into the goal. Happy days! Happy days!

The season 62-63 was what you might call a little different, as this was the winter of the big snow of 1963. Many matches had to be cancelled and fixtures could never be completed before the end of the season, so the league had to be split into four zones. Llanwddyn's zone was Llanrhaeadr, Llanfyllin, Llanfair, Llanwddyn. The champion of each zone played a semi-final and then a final.

As the seasons went by things got a little better as players became more plentiful. Players like Bernie Jones, big Peter Jones, little Peter Jones, Neil Carpenter, Terry Evans, the Tibbott brothers, etc. were very good young players. And there was Glyn Jones, I remember him writing to me when I was secretary asking when he could have a game.

One Saturday in the 60s we played in Llanrhaeadr and the team was:

| | |
|---|---|
| Goal | Bernie Jones |
| RB | Ian Jones |
| LB | E. Williams |
| RH | Little Peter Jones |
| CH | John Jones |
| LH | Meirion Jones |
| OR | Eric Jones |
| IR | Ray Jandrell |
| CF | Peter Jones, No 7 |

IL     Gwil Jones
OL    Henry Jones

Even the ref was a Jones — John Jones of Garthmyl — Bob Jones ran the line for Llanrhaeadr and I ran the line for Llanwddyn.

In the 1962-63 season I took over as the Secretary of the Llanwddyn Football Club from David Rowlands. David by now had the honour of being made Chairman of the MAL — a position he held for around twenty seasons.

When I was with the club I was very keen; football came first and after a match I prepared for the next. I never missed a match for fifteen seasons, home or away. I ran the line for ten seasons and at one time I selected the team.

The club started to get better around the mid 60s. We started to get a number of good young players by now, like Bernie Jones, Terry Evans, the Tibbott brothers, Neil Carpenter, big Peter Jones, little Peter Jones, Gwil Jones and the one and only Glyn Jones.

Clubs like Llanfyllin were in and out of the MAL a number of times and I managed to sign four good players from Llanfyllin for two seasons — David and Brian Roberts and Gareth and Mick Evans, Rhiwfawr.

I must not forget the good players we had to thank in forming the team in the run up to winning the league; players like Henry Jones, David Rowlands, Elwyn Williams, J. D. Hughes, Eric Jones, John Jones, G. O. Jones No 7, to name a few.

When you think about our little team, the season we won the league we beat Llansantffraid away 2-1 and look at Llansantffraid now!

The season 1971-72 we went on to win the MAL, also runners up in the village cup, played at Berriew.

After winning the league the club started to decline due to

Llanfyllin coming back into the league and good young players opting out to play for Mid Wales clubs, and two going to college.

Les Tibbott went on to play for Ipswich and under 23s for Wales.

A few more seasons went by and I had too much work to do at home so I could not get to all the matches, which left me a bit despondent with football.

Players by now had come back from Mid Wales and other MAL clubs, to play for Llanwddyn. The parting of the ways between secretary and club came in the 1979-80 AGM. What I wanted for the coming season was a loyal side, but what the players wanted was a winning side. But, what I can always say is I loved every game that Llanwddyn played — win, lose or draw.

*Llanwddyn Football Club, 1970.*

I will tell you a few humorous times I had with the football club. Starting with David Rowlands, as secretary of the club and David, chairman of the then MAL. I as secretary, travelled to league meetings with David in his Land Rover, firstly to Caerhowell, Montgomery and later that year, Wynnstay Llanfair C.

I think it must have been the league AGM I remember it was a nice summer evening and just before the Welshpool roundabout, an old chap on a bicycle was riding towards Welshpool watching the rabbits playing in the field. As we approached from behind he went off the road and fell off into the ditch. David being a polite sort of a chap, said, "I think I had better stop Bri and see if he's OK."

As we picked him up out of the ditch he was laughing and said "I was just watching the rabbits playing in the field."

Now David was not one to hang about when he was driving and liked to give the Land Rover a bit of clog. We were coming home from a meeting a very dark, wet night, just the other side of Ty-Crewen on the bad bends. Dave swerved and said, "Good God Brian, what was that?" What it was, was the old man of Pwynt going home from the pub on a black horse with a big black raincoat on without a light.

Staying with David years ago, we had to play on Grwnoer fields, where the shed is now, because the football field was being drained. It must have been early in the season because it was very hot and we were playing Llansantffraid. The game had to be stopped because a man from Manchester had drowned in the lake. Mr Butler, the Water Department foreman, told David, or I think David must have told him, "If he has drowned, I can't do

114

anything about it," and carried on playing.

Away to Kerry, first game of the season, playing in long grass, David loses his glasses and the ref stops the game to look for them.

Away to Trewern, ref stops the game, Roy Kelly's choking on a mint imperial.

Now Henry Jones had a lovely way of catching a player from behind when in full flight with a nice touch. We had a game one evening against Llangynog and Henry had caught Barry Paterson a few times with this little trip and I think Barry was an old rugby player. Before the end, he had had enough and sure enough he really caught Henry, and I being the ref thought he was really badly hurt. I stopped the game and they carried Henry off the field on an old ladder which we used for the nets. They got him to Dafarn, where he gets off the ladder and runs to the dressing room.

Away to Forden; Grand National Day. Henry playing outside left and leaves a wireless on the touch line and every time the ball went out of play or a goal kick he would go and listen to the race.

Away to Trewern, an enamel bucket of tea would be left in the stand with a bag of plastic cups. At half time, each player would have to dip his cup into the bucket for his drink, just imagine what it was like when you went for another cup. Yuck!

Once I fell out with a ref, Dai Williams it was, I know he cost us a vital game so I was not very pleased and got him in the dressing room after the match. I was really having a go at him, but the funny part about it was, I had the cheque to pay him and asked him what the fee was. I was writing out the cheque whilst having another go at him. I told him that he wasn't much good as a player when he played for Llanfechain but he was a damn sight worse referee. Anyway, by now I forgot how much the fee was to write on the cheque and I am sure he put another 50p on his fee when I asked him again.

The week after, he bought ten ewes from me in Llanfyllin and came and asked me for some luck money, but I told him to beggar off!

In the early days of football in Llanwddyn, transportation was more difficult to home and away games than it is today; not so many players had cars to travel in.

Before I passed my test in the car I had an Areal Header motorcycle and I used to travel to Pen-y-bont-fawr to pick up Bernie and go back to collect Plenydd Evans from Penygarnedd. Once I carried both of them; one across the tank and the other on the pillion. Sometimes I went to collect Fred from Llanerfyl as well.

Then I passed my test in the van, a little Ford van I had at first.

Meirion Jones from Llangynog carried the players from Llangynog but if Mei did not play I collected them. One time I carried seven players in my van. Bernie, Eric, Gwil, Glyn, John Jones Mount Quarry, Elgar Hughes and Plen.

One time I had a puncture but I didn't have a jack so Elgar and Bernie lifted the van while I changed the wheel.

To away games we had Maldwyn, Tommy Davies' bus which at one time used to be full. We used to run a draw to help pay for the bus at one time, twenty fags or a box of chocolates.

Maldwyn was himself very fond of football and we were very lucky to have his services which were very cheap.

I have an old bill in front of me; a bill I received on 29th April 1980 (not that long ago): Montgomery and return: Received £5.56; Balance £13.64. How much would it cost today?

One very wet day we were on the bus and above me there was a leak dripping on my head, so I picked up someone's brolly to save getting wet, but I was told off by Margaret Glanrhyd (a schoolgirl then) for upsetting her dad's bus.

I travelled to away matches for about twenty years but I never remember the bus breaking down!

This is my last story about Llanwddyn FC but I will finish with a few more light-hearted instances. Away to Guilsfield early in the season, arrived at the pitch while players changed. Around the pitch mushrooms were growing everywhere. I like mushrooms, so I collected a hatful. But, you see, these mushrooms had been planted and the ones growing on the pitch had been collected before the game, but the rest of the field had been left. The lady who rented the field came along, took the mushrooms off me and told me off.

Away to Aberystwyth Town in the Welsh Cup. A very wet Saturday and the field was like a bog after about one hour's play. Elwyn Williams broke his nose and I was Llanwddyn sponge man and ran onto the field in shoes to treat Elwyn, but one of my shoes came off in the mud and while I was putting my shoe back on, the Aber trainer shot past me and beat me to the job.

Incidentally, Aber beat us on that day but in the next round they played Wrexham at the Race Course. We had a bus load to Wrexham to watch the game, but Aber lost to Wrexham. It just shows how high a standard of football was played at that time.

Away to Llansantffraid when Big Peter Jones first started to play for Llanwddyn. Llansantffraid were a good team and Llanwddyn were just on the up, and I remember Digger Worrell in the Saints goal rolling the ball to Peter and saying "Have a go son" but we still did not score.

A few very good players not mentioned in my stories: Graham Evans, Alwyn Jones, Neil Carpenter, Phil Thomas, J. D. Hughes, John Tanfron, Charlie and Elwyn Groes, Brian Parry, Ian Jones, Ray and Fred Carpenter, Tony Smith, Terry Evans, Gwyn O. Jones No 7, to name but a few.

I first started to visit Llanwddyn in 1953, from Hirnant. I started by coming to the pictures on Friday nights with Phil and Margaret on the motorcycle and sidecar. Phillip soon got tired of the pictures and I started coming on my bicycle.

As I understand, pictures started in Llanwddyn after the war. Firstly in the old Legion Hall in the top village where the old dryer used to be. It was run by two brothers who bought a projector after coming out of the army and went round the villages each week. After the Community Centre was built, they came to the hall and had a screen at the back of the stage. They came to the centre for a few years until the governing body bought their own, due mainly to money collected from ballroom dances and hops run by John Derek Evans, Eddie Thomas, John Thomas, etc., dancing mainly to record music but I do remember Billy Gibson's Broadcast Band, as they were called and they came from Whitchurch.

The hall used to be quite full on Friday nights and the projectionists were Brian Roberts, Owen Butler and Ken Lloyd, taking turns every three weeks until Brian asked me whether I would like to help as he was now a family man and wanted to retire. Owen married and the same thing happened and so did Ken. So now I was left to run the pictures each week on my own.

Taken at random, from a few old diaries which I have kept since 1947 are a few pictures shown at Llanwddyn over the years:

| April 12th 1957 | "The Wooden Horse" |
| Feb 20th 1959 | "Goodbye My Lady" |
| Dec 30th 1960 | "The Siege at Pinchet" |
| Feb 10th 1961 | "The Moonrakers" |

Feb 2nd 1962      "Westbound" "Cowboy"
Jan 29th 1965     "Carson City"

After the pictures were finished each Friday the films had to be rewound and put into spool boxes and packed ready for posting after the show. I think Mr Emlyn Jones the headmaster and warden at the time, selected the films which we could afford. A lot of fun was to be had on film night because a governing body member was in charge each week to take money at the door, also try to keep the kids quiet which was quite a job when the film broke down or you had to change reels. Stamping of feet could be heard up into the projection room. The only governing body member who could keep the kids quiet was David Rowlands, all David had to do was walk down the hall once and you could hear a pin drop.

As more householders had TV less people came to the pictures. I can remember the only adult turning up was the late Sim Carpenter jnr. In the end I was taking money at the door, selling raffle tickets for a box of chocs and then running the film. Some times I was taking more money on the raffle. Films got very poor towards the end. I think the last film I put on was "King Kong". The projector is still in the centre and as far as I know is still in working order.

To get to the projector room you had to go into the gent's toilet, then up a ladder through a trap door and along two planks to get to the little room. I got used to going up and down after a few years. After a while I would start the film, go downstairs and watch the film in the hall, then run back upstairs before the reel had finished. One or two nights I dropped a clanger by staying down too long and the reel had run out — a lot of stamping of feet and singing — "Why are we waiting". One Friday night I had forgotten to put the catch on the pick-up reel and when I went upstairs the reel had dropped off and left a big pile of film on the floor. You would never believe how much film went on to a reel.

I used to get a few visitors to the projector room from time to time, mostly Master Berwyn Lloyd and Leonard Hughes, until one was either pushed or missed his footing on the planks and put his foot through the ceiling. They stopped coming for a while because I had a catch put on the trap door. By the way, who used to take the ladder away from time to time?

We had a few old films which had been given from time to time and I used to put them on for the kids after the Christmas Party, after changing at work and then going to join the party in the canteen before putting on the film show. Children who had not started school came to the party and I can tell you Mr Williams had his work cut out looking after them.

After the films came to an end in the village due mainly to TVs, something else had to be done for the village children. In the early 60s I went on to the governing body committee to help to organise entertainment in the community centre. I was already involved with the football club on Saturdays but became more involved in the centre. I was caretaker for a short while after the late Edwin Jones died, helping Mrs Jones with everyday work until Raymond took over as full-time caretaker.

A youth club was started before the days of the Aelwyd, two nights a week, summer and winter. In the summer months we had table tennis and badminton in the hall and stage and tennis outside on the court.

I have a bill in front of me from J. Ellis: Bill £28 paid for new table tennis table on 12/4/67.

We used to have as many as twenty children a night at one time paying 6p per night.

21/3/67 members present — Myself, Neil Carpenter, Terry Evans, Berwyn Lloyd, Philip Thomas, Ann Jones, Jean Jones, Judy Evans, Sandra Griffiths, Roger Morris, Jeff Carpenter, Len Hughes, Mair Williams, Peter Jones, Margaret and Mailys Glanrhyd, Tudor Hughes, Charles Shorey, Geraint Jones, Susan Griffiths and Helen Jones.

17/11/67, half a dozen table tennis balls 7/-.

These are other members who used to attend: Mike Hughes, Mr and Mrs D. Rowlands, Carol Evans, Jean Evans, Gwyneth Cowney, Clive Williams, Kevin Williams, Mervyn Hughes, Alan Hughes, Meinir Jones, David Vaugham, T. J. Jones, Irwin, Maggie Williams, Rhiannon Jones, Gwenda Jones, Olwyn Jones,

Kath Carsley, Thelma Jones, Ron Hill, Sandra Hill, Heulwen Wilcock and Roger Butler.

Wednesday night, it was badminton for the adults and paid-up members. We did play matches, home and away and would have done well in a badminton league but we were short of ladies or older girls.

Neil, D. Rowlands, Peter Jones, Berwyn Lloyd and myself were the male players who played in matches and the ladies were Mrs Rowlands, Ann Jones and Sandra Griffiths but we were always short of ladies to play. Neil went on to be a very good player.

Then I purchased an air rifle and bell target from Alexanders of Welshpool and started an air rifle club, and again would have done very well but you could not get enough people interested for away matches.

I was in Llanwddyn five nights a week in the hall and every Saturday with the football club. Mr Price, the PT instructor at the time in Llanfyllin came to take indoor football and PT in the main hall for a while and go camping in the summer.

A lot has gone on in the centre over the years. The club room in its hey-day, if you were not in the club room before 7 p.m. to put your name down for a game, you would be too late to have a game that night. Henry, Gwyn, etc. would be waiting for Edwin Jones to open up the club room at 6.30 every night.

Billiards was the only game played in the 60s/70s until snooker was seen on TV. Now a game of billiards is very rarely played. I never played billiards and snooker. I always said it was an old man's game but regret not leaning to play because it seems a very relaxing game. Again, Llanwddyn were in a billiards league in the 50s/60s and the shield is still in the centre, being the last team to win the league before it was disbanded. Henry, Gwyn, Fred Wilcox, T. J. Jones, etc., were in the team who played in the league.

Now the youth club went well until Mr Emlyn Jones the warden, headmaster at the time, wanted to start the Aelwyd and this is how it came to an end. I used to purchase crisps and pop from the Queens in Oswestry, much cheaper than in the shops and was able to sell them at the club for 1p profit per item for the club funds, until the local shopkeeper at the time complained to the warden, saying I was taking their trade selling pop and crisps. The warden came round to the hall and told me to stop this trade because the children were leaving litter about the place. In my opinion, this was untrue and a means of him running the club as an Aelwyd, but the Aelwyd was never as popular as the youth club. Too much red tape and rules.

The football club is the only thing that has lasted in the village for the young. Years ago annual tournaments were held in the centre, billiards, snooker, table tennis, badminton, air rifle, dominoes, darts and even draughts. Shields and cups were purchased and a finals night was quite a big occasion. Henry won the double for four years, billiards and table tennis. He was very good.

I cannot see the centre ever being the same again. It is the same in every village, more people go to the pubs, TV and discos today and the population has declined as well. Around Abertridwr, families of five to six children were quite common, having more than three today would be classed as a large family.

In 1967 I thought it was time I started to think about getting a young lady. I was now thirty-three and getting a little long in the tooth. I started writing to June through selling her a Lassie Collie pup. This was mid 1967. June told me she lived on a smallholding called Sweethills near Cheadle, Staffs. She had been left by her husband with three boys and a baby girl twelve months old. Her mum and dad lived on a farm in Cheadle and helped her rear her young family as she had been left without a penny. All she had was a cow which she milked for the house.

We wrote to each other for quite a while. I told her I sold a lot of puppies and Phillip bred pedigree Lassie Collies. This breed, it seems was June's favourite and asked if Phil would sell her a pup. This was how we first met. June wrote to say she could collect the pup one weekend.

One lovely summer's day in 1968 June came with Antonette and friends Dot and Walley Edwards. I lived at Brwynen at this time and it was a very warm Sunday and it seems June had told Walley if she liked me to leave her and go with Dot to the seaside for the rest of the day, if she didn't, wait while she had a chat and collected the pup. It seems she liked what she saw and off Walley and Dot went, to collect June later. June and Antonette, who was now three years old, a lovely blonde little girl, met Mum and Dad, Phil and Kath. June had bought a picnic lunch with her so I took them to the mountain with the Austin Cambridge Estate, the car I had at the time. June thought the views were wonderful. Antonette was very shy as I remember, hanging on to her mum and sucking her thumb.

At this time Jack Carsley was my mate on the saw at work and I was renting the grounds off him at Llechwedd-Du and grazing cattle there. Jack was leaving Llechwedd-Du to live at Bryn Vyrnwy in the top village. After June had finished her picnic we went for a ride to see the cattle at Llechwedd-Du. June loved the lake but we didn't go to Llechwedd-Du itself but we could see it from the lakeside. After a while I proposed to June saying, "If you will marry me, I will get you that lovely big house to live in."

June has always loved Llechwedd-Du and would not live anywhere else, but at this time she did not say she would marry me because she had four children and didn't think it fair for me to take on a family of that size. Anyway Walley collected her as planned plus the Lassie Collie pup and off they went.

After June got home her dad called and she told her dad all about her trip to Wales plus telling him about my marriage proposal. June's dad told her he would not always be there to look after her as he was getting older and if she loved me and I loved her and the children, it would be the best thing she could do. After June had been to Llechwedd-Du, we wrote to each other every day until we got married in July 1970.

Llechwedd-Du came up for rent after Jack had lived there for fifty-nine years. I was unlucky with my application at first but it was turned back and I had it at the second attempt. I had Llechwedd-Du for around ten months before we got married and I spent a lot of time there hedge laying, making fires in the house, etc. I took bags of offcuts from work for the fires each time I went up to the house. One Sunday I remember, being a very wet day, I lit six fires in the house, stocking up well before I left. What happened next you might ask. Well, we had gone to bed at Brwynen and the phone rang. Mr Quine said that Llechwedd-Du was on fire and that the fire brigade were damping down. It could have been far worse if Roy Kelly and Mr Quine had not passed down Bryn Gwyn Road and seen a glow in the house. By the time the brigade got there it was much worse of course.

What had happened was a beam in one bedroom went right

under the grate with only a slate to prevent a fire. With me stoking up before I left it got too hot and started to smoulder. We had a new bedroom floor and new kitchen ceiling plus bricking up all bedroom grates. We were very lucky.

Before we got married I went to Sweethills every two weeks, sometimes leaving home Friday after work, and staying Friday and Saturday night or leaving after football on Saturday, but I never missed a football match for fifteen years. I used to sleep at her mum and dad's house so I had to be in early or look out, "Where have you been till now?"

Each time I went down it would be six pork chops off Alf in Llanfyllin. That would be the weekend treat. Mick used to ask his mum, "Is Bri coming this weekend with his pork chops."

You would arrive at Sweethills, the lads covered in oil because they lived by a scrapyard and used to strip cars down for the owner and they seem to have done it ever since. Antonette would be about the yard or with her mum.

We were very lucky at the time we married, because we married in the school holidays, Mick had left school twelve months before and lived with his gran and went to work. David had just left school, Alan was moving up from primary to go to Llanfyllin and Antonette had not started school. Antonette went to play group when it first started for twelve months before starting school.

June came down for a week's holiday before we got married and stayed at Bwlch Sych, in a caravan. I didn't have much holiday left, so Phillip and Mum used to take June and Antonette to the seaside (safe enough).

We went to see Mr And Mrs Lewis, Sardis to arrange about getting married and fixed the big day; I think it was 20th July or near enough. A lovely day it was too, my brother Arthur from Blackpool was best man (Phil too shy). Terry Evans drove June to chapel and to the reception in the hall. Uncle Albert and June's mum brought a crate of champagne and we still have one bottle left. June's mum made the cake with two football teams for decoration on top. We never had a honeymoon as such but we all went back to Llechwedd-Du for a house warming party and I nearly got a rupture trying to carry June over the threshold, but we did have a good time even though we had a four children start.

We did have a few days out before settling down to married life. Mick went back to work and just left us with three children. We didn't have a lot of money but just had a day out here and there. I remember one day we went to Black Rock Sands and June beat us all in a race along the beach. Walking along the street in Porthmadog, Alan wanted a Dinky car but Mother said no. Alan put his head down and dragged his feet all the way along the town. Dave was very good, never asked for anything and Antonette was just a happy little girl.

The following June, Ian was born. To this day I don't know how it came about because we never had any lodgers, but I suppose it was only fair to have one of my own. Now the children are all married, a question mark by Ian, and we have twelve grandchildren and four great-grandsons. We have been married thirty years in July and still love one another very much.

On Friday evening, 4th February, I had the pleasure of going to watch the Tanat Theatre Club present a stage version of Lionel Bart's musical Oliver. Another superb performance, directed by Gaynor Richfield.

The stage was very well prepared by Revd Raymond Hughes. A cast of nearly fifty well-polished and disciplined children and adults put on a very good entertaining evening. People in the area are very lucky to have Gaynor and her stalwarts to be able to keep putting on these great shows. The last four shows were sell outs.

It was nice to see three locals in the show, Mr David Thomas and his two children Ffion and Hedd from Hafan Heulog. Bob Nightingale, Mick Morris, his daughter Sara and David Clark were all in the first show in 1982. Bob Nightingale has been in every show since 1982.

The Tanat Theatre Club was formed in 1982 by Edwyn and Gaynor Richfield, both actors in their own rights. Edwyn starred in films and TV. I myself was with the club for fourteen years and enjoyed every minute of it. When we first started we did the Good Old Days for three seasons and toured round the villages. Trevor Vaughan carrying the props round the shows in his little lorry.

We had a number of good singers in the early days but they are few and far between these days and that is why Gaynor turned more to stage shows and pantos. We have lost a lot of actors and singers such as Keith Wild, Nancy Stanton, Dot Williams, Janet Morris, etc. Gaynor is very strict to work with but very thorough, once you start to rehearse she seems as though she owns you. The casts are great to work with.

About twelve years ago we purchased the old Green School for rehearsals. A few years after we had a grant and were able to fit a second storey to keep the props and wardrobe. We are very lucky to have a stage crew, wardrobe ladies, pianists and Raymond Hughes who gives up so much of his time painting scenery and I must not forget Iris Green on the prompting.

I think the best shows have been — Under Milk Wood (twice), Cinderella and the Wizard of Oz, with Alwyn Williams playing the lead. Alwyn was a big loss to the club when he was made headmaster at Llangollen and called it a day; he was a great actor and fun to work with. Gaynor has not got the talent she did have but it is great to see them going and doing so well.

We did manage to get the Tanat Theatre Club twice to perform the Good Old Days and Murder at the Vicarage in the hall and I remember Edwyn and Gaynor telling me what a lovely hall and changing rooms we have in Llanwddyn, much more modern than in Llanrhaeadr. Since then Gaynor is on the hall committee in Llanrhaeadr and has got grants to extend the stage end for better changing rooms and lowered the ceiling to get better sound and better lighting.

Long may the Tanat Theatre Club live.

J

In 1976 we started our fold of Highland cattle with an incalf cow from JCB Farms Ltd., gradually building up to around thirty we have today. In the spring of 1986 we bred a young Dun bull which put us on the road to success, Berwyn 1st of Llechwedd-Du was his name, out of a good black cow, by Joseph of Cladick a white bull we purchased in Scotland.

We advertised Berwyn in our Newsletter *The Highland Journal*. Herr Von Heisler and his wife came over from Germany and bought him for £1,900. Berwyn was transported out to Germany and soon became farm use, siring many good young cattle. Berwyn was sold to Herr Hanst Friedrich Baumer who kept 600 breeding cows of five different breeds. Herr Baumer was loaded with money and had his own cattle market built. Berwyn finished his breeding days last year but I believe he is still alive.

The BSE trouble spoilt the trade of Highland cattle to Germany but we were lucky in having three good years exporting. This set us up right, I became a show judge and field officer for Wales and the border counties. In 1995 I was invited to Germany to judge and inspect Highlanders for the German members. Prior to going to Germany, a young bull damaged my knee with his horn but I never went to the doctors because of him sending me to hospital, but I suffered in Germany I can tell you. Allan took me to Manchester Airport to catch my flight but I had never flown before, but it was OK. From Manchester I flew to Heathrow and met Callum McDonald from Auch fold in Glencoe.

Now the Auch fold is owned by Lady Trevor from Chirk, and Callum knew the Oswestry area well. I learnt a lot from

Callum on the flight to Hamburg. At Hamburg Airport we were met by Marion Beat Naegeli of the Wartenberg fold where we had to inspect a Black Bull out of Berwyn of Llechwedd-Du. His name was Berwyn of Behrens a lovely bull of great length.

Storks built their nests on the chimneys of the house even though they had no children. The day before a keeper had shot a roe deer in the garden and that was to be our dinner.

We inspected her bull and he was passed and tattooed. Beat then took us round the cattle, all pets as they seem to be in Germany. One was a nice young cow called Hafina 1st of Llechwedd-Du.

We now went back to the house and Marion was preparing the roe deer in the kitchen ready for our dinner and I can tell you this, it was delicious as was the whole meal. With every dinner we had in Germany, we had cabbage and I know now why they call Germans, "Krauts".

We stayed one night with the Naegeli family, then we were taken to the fold of Herr Potthoff who incidentally sold Ivor Williams trailers in Oberberg. At the Oberberg fold we were to inspect tattoos which took us half the day. We then moved on to Herr Falko Steinberg's fold across the old Berlin Wall. Now Herr Falko asked Callum and myself whether we would like to go for a wild boar shoot before it went dark, so off we go with a rifle each, dropping each of us off at a hide in a tree. It was quite frightening really, stuck up a tree thinking 'Will he come back and pick me up?' It was getting dark now and you could hear the wild boar in the distance, but that was about all. It got really dark before Herr Falko picked us up. He did show us a big male boar in a freezer he had shot in the week and it must have been twenty score and hair about six inches long.

Our job the next day was to be picking and passing a bull out of twelve two-year-old bulls as Falko sold all his males as bull beef. But the night we arrived Falko and his wife had booked a meal on the outskirts of Berlin where we had wild boar for the main course, which was quite nice but all the meals in Germany seem to be stew. You cannot get a steak like we have at home. Berlin I found very drab and dirty.

Now the following morning, early, Callum chose a bull and I chose a bull out of the twelve bulls. Not a hard job really because a number of them had uneven horns. Falko decided to keep the two bulls so they were tattooed and loaded to go to Hamburg, which was our next job at an open day in Hamburg cattle market. Members from all over Germany brought cattle to be inspected and shown. We had to inspect each one and give the marks out of ten for head, legs, top and overall appearance.

One clever Dick of an old German doctor who kept a few cattle — and I should think didn't like British people telling him what to look for in Highlanders — didn't agree with what we were telling him about his cattle and he was told by the German President to be quiet and behave.

We were picked up at the show by Bill and Benna Smith, friends of ours, who had gone out to Germany to manage a fold for Herr Baumer who as I said had Berwyn of Llechwedd-Du.

What I found about Germany was everybody drove on the wrong side of the road and it seemed quite frightening when taking corners. This was to be the highlight of our visit.

When we arrived at Herr Baumer's it was very dark, but we were made very welcome by the Baumer family. Herr Baumer is a very rich man in the area of Westerhorn and buys all the farms in the area, making himself a very large estate. A seven-course evening meal was laid on for us. We sat down at the table at 7.30 p.m. and we were still eating and drinking at 10.30. Duck, I remember was the main course.

The following morning, Bill and Benna went to the German National Poultry Show in Hamburg so it was left for Herr Baumer and his wife to take us round his cattle. First a visit to see Berwyn and fifty cows. All the fields were divided with electric fences running off the mains. Miles and miles of fences no hedges.

Berwyn looked really well and very quiet. A few of the cows with him were cattle we had bred. Next were the Aubucks which 1 think were his best cattle. Next the Salains and beef Shorthorns and last the Galloways. This took most of the day with a stop for lunch at a hotel where the meal had been booked beforehand.

Herr Baumer then took us to his cattle mart, which is also his cattle headquarters and where all the cattle are halter trained. He then took us round all the young bulls in open yards all very new and posh.

It was now time to catch the flight home. Herr Baumer took us to Hamburg Airport to catch the flight to Heathrow and then to Manchester where Allan and June were waiting.

I enjoyed the visit very much but was not all that impressed with Germany. Give me the Welsh hills any day. Sadly Callum passed away last year with cancer. The only thing that spoilt the trip was my knee which slowed me down very much.

*Herr Von Heisler with Berwyn 1st*
*at Llechwedd-Du.*

Autumn show and sale of pedigree Highland at Oban livestock market on 12th and 13th October.

Michael, June and I set off for Oban at 10 a.m on Saturday 10th October, a journey of 410 miles. Quite a nice run with different kinds of weather along the way. We did have two short stops en route, arriving at the market at 6.45 p.m. but much to our surprise the lorry taking eighteen cattle for sale had unloaded the cattle and tied them in the pens before we arrived. Idwal Davies had also started at 10 a.m. from Llanfyllin with the cattle and had only one break of forty-five minutes at Carlisle. We could not believe he could have arrived before us with an artic. He must have flown.

We bedded the cattle down and fed them, went to our digs, a Mrs Eddie Hughes, where we have stayed for the last fifteen years. Sunday was spent washing and shampooing six cows and their calves. Michael took his mum for a ride to Fort William and it rained and rained. Sunday evening was spent at the society's AGM at the Alexander Hotel, Oban.

Monday was show day. Michael and his mum were watching the judging and taking down the results. I was helping to put the finishing touches to three cows and three calves I wanted to show. We are the only members who put Welsh names on our cattle, making them a little different. When it came to the class, 'Cows with calves at foot', Jeff took Glesni and her heifer calf Eilir Goch 4th of Llechwedd-Du, a twelve-year-old Dun cow with her calf. I took in Gwyneira 2nd a ten-year-old cow and her heifer calf Heulwen 4th of Llechwedd-Du. John Hepburn took

*Gwyneira 1st of Llechwedd-Du.*

*Gwyneira 2nd, Royal Show winner, 1990.*

in Bronwen 4th and her heifer calf Olwen 3rd of Llechwedd-Du. Out of two classes of twenty-four cows, Glesni finished fourth, very good for the oldest cow in the show.

The champion female was Capleadh 26th of Millerston, a white incalf three-year-old, bred by an eighty-four-year-old member, Mr Tom McLatchie and she went on to make 3,200 guineas, bought by a Mr Stubbs of Stafford, who also bought three more lots at over 1,500 guineas. Idwal took them home with what we bought, also Tudor Griffiths of Oswestry.

After the show which took nearly five hours, we had to get ready for the dinner and celigh at McTavishes Kitchen. Now when we got to McTavishes, there was no lift and two flights of stairs to climb. With June in her chair, I had to fetch six strong men, some in kilts, to carry June in her chair to the dance hall. They love this, they have carried her before and certain people collected her and have some fun. They also had her on the dance floor, in her chair, doing a Scottish dance, spinning her around. The meal was very good but it's the after dinner speeches that get a bit boring. The dance itself did not start until 10.45 and went on until 1 a.m. June was carried down the stairs after the dance with some a little worse for drink but she got to the car in one piece OK.

Tuesday was sale day, with some heifers selling well and some very poor. Top price was 3,200 guineas but you could get a good two-year-old heifer for 150. Our cows and calves sold very well with Gwyneira and Henlwen making over 1,000 guineas each. We also bought an incalf three-year-old heifer and a six-month-old heifer calf for replacements. It was a very good sale but the steers were selling very poorly.

We left Oban early Wednesday morning and went through Glen Orchy, it was beautiful following the River Orchy for about ten miles. Men were standing in the river salmon fishing. We stayed in Callander for the last night and did last minute shopping. We started for home Thursday morning at 9.30 and arrived home at 3.30 p.m., took the hired estate car back to Welshpool and that was it for another year.

Leicestershire County Show. On Monday morning, V-E Day at 6.15 a.m., June and myself set off with our son Allan to judge Highland cattle classes at Leicester County Show.

We arrived at the showground at 9.15 a.m. on a cold windy morning. I met my class steward Mr Don Johnson at 10 a.m. ready to start to judge five classes of very good Highlanders. Fifty cattle forward on the day.

Class 1 — Yearling Bull: 1st Mrs Dawes — Bacchus of Craycombe; 2nd Mr Miller — William 3rd of Weetwood; 3rd Mrs Dawes — Fury 4th of Craycombe.

Class 2 — Senior Bull: 1st D. Haighton — Domhnull of Ellerdine; 2nd D. Owen — McGreggor; 3rd Mrs Goadby — Black Prince 2nd of Rigg.

Class 3 — Yearling Heifer: 1st Mrs Dawes — Little Lady of Craycombe; 2nd D. Owens — Lynette; 3rd Lady Martin — Rwanda.

Class 4 — 2 yr old Heifer: 1st Mrs Dawes — Jonquil of Craycombe; 2nd Mr Rainey — Corrigal of April; 3rd Mrs Barr — Little Lady of Craycombe.

Class 5 — Cow with Calf at Foot: 1st Mrs Dawes — Capladh of Craycombe; 2nd Lady Martin — Regina of the Brand; 3rd Lady Martin — Faoicte of the Brand.

Pairs: 1st Mr Rainey; 2nd Mrs Dawes.

My show champion was a very well grown two-year-old white heifer from Mrs H. L. Dawes of Worcestershire with Jonquil of Craycombe and my reserve was a big three-year-old red bull from Mr D. Haighton of Hodnet, Shropshire with Domhnull of Ellerdine.

From the showground we went another twenty-five miles to Hucknell, Nottinghamshire to spend a couple of hours with our son Ian.

Leaving Hucknell at 6.30 p.m. for home to finish the night at the V-E Day dance in the community centre.

*Judging at Northallerton.*

Lichfield Sale — the recession in farming has really started to bite, hitting every aspect of the industry. I can understand why farmers and their wives have to find part-time jobs to make ends meet. Our Highland cattle, which I must say, have bought us in a lot of money over the last twenty years, have now slumped to less than what we paid for our first cattle in 1975.

This year we decided to sell our annual surplus of cattle at the Highland Cattle Society Sale at Lichfield Market on Saturday 25th September. This was to save the long haul of the cattle to Scotland. As the prices turned out, a good job we did. The Thursday and Friday before the sale I spent washing four cows, three calves, two yearling heifers and they all looked very nice when Idwal and Shirley Davies came to collect them.

All our cattle have Welsh Christian names and our fold prefix is Llechwedd-Du. The first cow led into the lorry was Hafina 3rd of Llechwedd-Du, this was a red nine-year-old cow which I was reluctant to sell. She has been my show cow for the last five years but was a little small for the major shows. Then came Rhain 5th an old white cow, she was twelve years old and starting to show her age. Followed by Megan a yellow cow six years old but not my type of Highland cow. The last cow in was Rhiannon 4th, a young four-year-old red cow who had lost her calf in the summer but was sold because we still have twenty cattle in the fold.

Idwal loaded, it was time to load our trailer which our Mick was taking for us. Two bull calves, Sioned 2nd and then the yearling heifers. Sioned 1st and Awena 2nd. Hay, straw, buckets, meal, etc., in the back of the pick-up and he was ready for the off. Now, the job of loading June into the Astra and clothes for the weekend.

We set off for Lichfield at 3.30 and arrived at the market at 6.30 and unloaded the cattle. A beef dinner was laid on by the Midland & South of England Club and was enjoyed by around thirty members. Time after the dinner was spent feeding and watering the cattle and tucking them in for the night. Mick went home with the pick-up but June and I slept in the car. June was too warm and I was too cold, just can't win!

Up early on Saturday morning, Idwal helping me to feed, Shirley looking after June and then a lovely breakfast in the market canteen. Showing the cattle was at 10 a.m., so time was spent grooming and putting linseed oil on the cows' horns. Hafina was the only cow I was showing and came fourth in her class. The sale was to commence at 12.30, so before the sale we had dinner.

A sale of pedigree Charolais was held first which was a disaster,

*June with two young bulls. The one on the left went to Denmark, the other to the Isle of Rhum*

with very little cattle sold, lovely two-year-old heifers only making 400 guineas. I was dreading going into the ring because I was the first in with Rhiannon, but in I went and who should buy Rhiannon but Idwal so she went back to Llanfyllin for 250 guineas. The four cows averaged 250 guineas. We had to sell because we have so many. The yearling heifers we bought home because we were only offered fifty guineas each for them. Still a better sale than the Charolais, because two two-year yellow heifers made 1,400 guineas and 3,400 guineas, both to the same buyer, bought for showing next year. Idwal had bought another heifer, loaded them and our two unsold heifers, had tea and started for home at 4.30.

We are very lucky with our fold because all our cattle bar two have been bred by ourselves and don't cost much to feed. Not like the continentals which cannot winter without dipping into meal bags and we all know how much that costs. We only feed meal when showing and getting them ready for sales. People who have paid big money for cattle five or six years ago, they are the ones who are suffering. For instance, one man selling two cows at the sale for 300 guineas and 350 guineas had paid 4,000 guineas and 2,500 guineas for them five years ago.

In the spring of 1976 the Llechwedd-Du fold of pedigree Highland cattle was formed. People up and down the country still say to me why do you keep Highland cattle and not Welsh Blacks? There are a number of reasons why we keep them, but the main reason was that in the early days I had worked in the forestry for twenty-eight years and found feeding and cleaning out cattle in the winter months was getting a bit too much as I had to be at work for 8 a.m. plus the fact we have two farms five miles apart, but the best thing I ever did was to take early retirement in the mid 80s.

Our other farm, Brwynen, is where most of our cattle are kept and is the larger of the two. The farmhouse stands at 1,200 feet rising to 1,400 feet where the cattle are grazed for most of the year.

Starting with one cow like a lot of other members we purchased an aged cow from the Lakeside fold, Raoghnailt Ile 6th and incalf to Diarmad Ile 2nd. Our first calf was born out of this cow with the Llechwedd-Du prefix; Alastair 1st of Llechwedd-Du. Raoghnailt went on to have two heifers, Antonette and Bethan of Llechwedd-Du which have both been sold in the last two years. Raoghnailt is now thirteen years of age and still going strong. We then purchased two heifers from Mr Swain's Crossways fold, Church Stretton out of Ardmenish cows by a big yellow bull, Gille-A-Gleann of Douglas, bought in Oban for 1,000 guineas in the early 1970s.

We are now up to ten breeding cows and a stock bull plus followers getting up to thirty cattle at times. We run the cattle with 130 Welsh breeding ewes plus lambs in the season.

I must tell you a story about Joseph of Cladich, our first bull. We bought Joseph at the Oban Spring Sale from David Fellowes. Cladich as a bull calf and he is now a legend on the Isle of Mull. There was something about Joseph I will never forget.

After getting him passed by the society and running with the cows to produce three crops of calves he has left us with five cows in the fold plus granddaughters. When the time came to change our stock bull Joseph was too big for my stock trailer so I caught him in the middle of the field and walked him home five miles; it took me three hours. You see Joseph only had a bottom gear and must have had the brake on. We took Joseph to the Oban Spring Sale with some other cattle and on the way up the M6 we had to stop on the hard shoulder as Joseph had one of his horns sticking out through the air vents half-way across the motorway. There will never be another Joseph I still miss him very much.

The following spring we were again in Oban selling a white cow and a red bull by Joseph. At the sale we met Neil and asked him about Joseph. "Come over to Mull and see him. I will meet you in my car at Craignure and take you to see him." The following morning we set sail for the island where we were met by Neil and taken to see the legend of Mull. He was on his own and let me put my arm around his big neck. Joseph will always be remembered in Wales as the Big White Bull.

All our cattle now have Welsh names which June studies from her little Welsh name book. These are Celtic names. Tomas of Benmore our last stock bull was very hardy and if you look at the stock bull list in the *Journal* you will find more Benmore bulls than any other. If you see where Judy Bowser lives you will understand the reason for deep bodies and short legs. We do not like big leggy cows.

Our stock bull at the moment is Brinsley Billy of Austin. Someone said to me "I would not buy a bull with a name like that," but look at his pedigree Douneside, lie, Ulva, Lakeside, Skipness, etc.

June has studied bloodlines and with careful selection you could buy bulls without inbreeding for forty years. Study bloodlines and you won't go far wrong, and don't buy bad walkers. A good head, level back and four good legs make a good Highlander. Crop ear in our opinion is a bad defect. Keep it going and you will end up without ears. Any crop eared calves born in our fold will be out and if I am asked to judge any show it will also be a fault.

We go to Scotland to the sales and see big fat bulls which would not and could not serve a cow weeks after purchase. What good would that be if you took the bull home and found a cow bulling the following day? You would have to wait three weeks for the bull to slim down. I understand that bulls are kept inside for months before bringing them to a sale. How can you expect them to walk well when they have had little exercise? If I bought one of them it would be dead within a week — too nesh for our

*Joseph of Cladich before he went to Scotland.*

144

part of the world.

We have nearly a week at the Royal Show with the cattle and the time seems to fly. Bill and Bina Smith seem to make all the competitors so welcome at the show. At nights we have a few drinks, with the cattle, sitting on straw bales telling tales and having a singsong. I found it a great honour to be asked to judge in my first show season. I judged at five shows one of which was the important Devon County Show.

Having June by my side with the same interest as myself I am very happy and grateful with my life the way it has turned out. But most of all our Highland cattle mean everything to me.

K

# Postscript

I have not written any magazine stories since August 2001, due mainly to my wife and I being in and out of hospital since 29th December, 1994, but I would like to bring you up to the present day.

In November, 1994, I had my left knee damaged by a young Highland bull. I went into the building to collect my buckets which he liked to push around his pen. On picking up the buckets he thought I wanted to play. He swung his head and caught me in the knee joint with his horn. He never even broke the skin, but I could tell by the pain it had done a lot of damage, it did not hurt a lot at the time but started to hurt later.

I didn't go to see my doctor because I was going to judge Highlanders in Germany, my first trip in a plane as well.

In Germany my knee got worse because I did a lot of walking. Not only was I judging but also going around different folds assessing bulls. The last bull I inspected was in the old East Germany. As I remember we passed over the Berlin Wall which had been taken down by then.

The road was very rough because with it being on the border they were falling out over who should repair the road.

Instead of resting my leg, I walked miles. I did a lot of damage to my knee.

After arriving home the following week I had to go to Scotland, to the old Conservative Prime Minister, Sir Alex Douglas-Home's fold, Douglas and Angus Estate at Douglas just outside Glasgow, to assess two two-year-old bulls.

My leg hurt very badly this day, and after doing my duty we went back home. Luckily my son Allan and June were with me. Allan driving our car as I could not use the clutch owing to my left leg. I could not drive by now, so we bought a little Corsa automatic which means you never use your left leg because automatics don't need a clutch.

What had happened was the bull's horn caught me in the joint of my left knee, shattering the bones inside. This had caused the broken bones to grind together, hence lasting damage.

I still didn't go to the doctor because I thought I was getting better — a big mistake.

As the weeks went by I was always feeling pain but not bad enough to stop me working.

As time went by my leg started to swing from side to side, caused by bone inside my knee getting ground away.

Christmas had been and gone by now. I was acting in A Christmas Carol at this time with the Tanat Theatre Club. Sunday evening, December 29th 1994, we were going to a dress rehearsal and I wanted to get ready to go. This was the start of a very long illness, nine years in fact. June asked whether I had fed her budgies. I had not, so despite it was pouring down with rain I went out without a coat. I slipped with my right leg, taking all the weight on my left, which snapped just below the knee causing a compound fracture.

I lay in the water in terrible pain, unable to move. I shouted to June to tell her what had happened. June was in a wheelchair by now so could not get to me. She phoned our eldest son who lives on our other farm to tell him to phone for the ambulance, and to come up to help as I was in terrible pain.

Mick came first but I could not move because of the pain. I could feel the water passing under me and I was very cold. Mick covered me with blankets until the ambulance arrived.

Sure enough it arrived. Paramedics came to me but I would not let them touch me. They got an inflatable stretcher around me and lifted me into the ambulance. I was shouting in pain, very cold and wet.

Off to the Shropshire Orthopaedic Hospital at Gobowen, near

Oswestry. June and Mick followed with dry clothes and things I needed in hospital.

The compound fracture had caused internal bleeding which made the X-ray very dark.

I went onto Kenyon Ward and was treated for a broken leg. June and Mick stayed with me for a while. I was hanging onto June with pain. I counted every ten seconds a surge up my leg and gritted my teeth when I got to nine.

As days went by the pain got less but the damage to my knee did not show up because of the dark X-rays.

While I was in hospital the production of A Christmas Carol was started. They allowed me to go to the opening show. David, our second son, and June took me to the show in a wheelchair. I was also on arm sticks by now and able to get into the car, but had to be pushed into the hall by wheelchair.

I was made very welcome by all the other actors and people in the hall. The Rev Kit Carter, a very clever man, had filled in for my two parts very well. I was presented with a large box of chocolates by Gaynor Richfield.

I was told by the hospital staff to be back in hospital before twelve o'clock. Like Cinderella when the clock struck twelve I was tucked up in my bed.

I slept downstairs for a while after being discharged; June in her wheelchair and me in the bed.

I got better very quickly but could tell my knee was very bad. We had help on the farms until I was off arm sticks.

It was March 1995 by now and I went to the Outpatients at the hospital. The damage was found in my knee on the X-rays. I was told by Professor Richerson that I needed a temporary knee replacement. When I took the weight on my right leg, I could swing my leg from side without any pain. The professor showed me on the X-rays what had happened. There was a hole on the outside of my knee where the bull had caught me. It was caused by bone wasting. Even though I was told about the knee replacement I had to wait until May 1996 for the operation.

What the professor did for the temporary job was to fill my knee with what he called 'cement' to stop my leg swing.

In May 1997, a year later, after having two heart attacks, I needed an angioplasty operation. This means putting a stent-like valve inside the artery. This was done without being put out because you have to be awake while they do the job. I watched it being done on a monitor. It is a very clever op, starting in your groin, and like a little wire it went to your heart and you could follow it on the screen. A stent was inserted.

Going back to my knee jobs. I did not have much luck because the first one went wrong and an infection had got into it causing me to go yellow. I was put on a drip to drain off the rubbish.

The first operation was done on a Tuesday, the second was done on the following Tuesday, so you can tell I had quite a lot of stick.

Barbara, one of June's carers, brought June to see me every day for five weeks.

On discharge the professor told me they would have to keep an eye on me because he thought the infection could return.

Sure enough it did later. Even though my knee kept swelling and was hot the professor discharged me in May 1999, and said to come back in 2001.

For two years I used to phone the hospital quite often because of pain and I could not bend my knee. I was told to wait for my appointment on the 5th May 2001.

I knew the professor would have a shock when he saw the X-rays, and sure enough you could see on the X-ray a gap on the knee bone just like a bite out of an apple.

The professor and a physio came to me and said this would be the end of my farming, and to try and lose weight (I don't know what that had to do with the case).

He turned me over to Dr Spencer Jones, the surgeon who does what they call 'redos'.

A week later my daughter, who used to clean for her mum from time to time, came after me outside and told me she had received a phone call from the SOH, telling me they had a cancellation and would I like to go and see Spencer Jones that same afternoon. I thought that sounded odd, wanting to see me after only one week, when they had been making me wait two years, but I did go.

Sure enough there were eight nurses and a doctor waiting for me. This was no cancellation I can tell you! They were in a flap after seeing what had been done by leaving me for two years. An infection had been left dormant in my knee and had flared up and more or less eaten my knee away.

They made me very welcome and looked at me as much as to say "Poor old bugger." Spencer Jones pulled his chair right up to me and told me I would likely have to have my leg amputated, but they would try to save it with two ops.

The first op was to remove all my knee joint to get rid of the infection. They put in what they called a spacer. This was to be done in September 2001.

They sent me home very confused and worrying that I might have to have my leg chopped off.

I went for what they call a pre-med before the op to make sure you are fit to have the op done. I went through all this procedure and the last test was done on my heart. I was uptight as you can tell; my heart was going bump, bump, bump. The test was not very good after having two heart attacks.

I then had to meet Spencer Jones in the consulting room. He said "I am sorry Mr Dawson but I am not willing to do the operation because I don't want to end up with a dead body on the table." So that was that.

I did not give up. I went private at the Nuffield in Shrewsbury. I went by taxi from the nursing home in Welshpool as I did not know the venue; it was easier that way.

I saw a heart surgeon, a Mr Waldridge, who gave me a number of tests and told me my heart was good enough to stand the ops and he would write to Spencer Jones and tell him so.

I did not hear from the hospital and my leg was getting worse as was the pain. I kept phoning the hospital and was always told the same story — I had been put on the waiting list but could not be told when I would have the operation.

I got fed up with this, but I had been told to try Mick Bates, our Liberal MP. I did just that and sure enough Mick Bates sent me a copy of the letter he had sent to Spencer Jones.

A week later I was sent an appointment to go for a pre-med. This was in the spring of 2001.

When I was waiting for the doctor to come and meet me I had had other tests by then. The doctor said as he came into the room "Oh you are the expensive patient are you!"

"What do you mean?" said I.

"Well the component to be inserted into you is costing around £10,000."

I jumped up and told him "It is not my fault, you have made the cock-ups, not me!"

"Don't be like that, I only thought you would like to know!"

I told him he could have told me in a kinder manner.

He did say he was sorry and carried on to tell me what was to be done. He had made an appointment for the first operation in June and the second one in November, both in 2002.

You see how your MP can help you in the times of need!

June soon came and the op went very well and I was soon ready to sit out in a chair. But just as the last quota of antibiotic was fed into my left arm (inserted at 2.30 a.m.), more trouble for Brian again. I felt ill when I awoke. I felt as if I was on fire and was itching all over. I could not see myself because of the dimmed night lights. I did not call a nurse but I felt very ill.

A nurse did come to check my drip and I told her I felt ill. She put on the main light, looked at me and then ran. I then passed out.

When they did wake me up there were seven doctors and nurses around ready to wire me up.

One doctor was inserting a needle into my wrist, another doctor was putting a drip tube in my left arm. I already had a needle left in after my op. A nurse was taking my blood pressure and temperature. When the doctors saw my temperature I have never seen doctors move so quickly. It was 102° and I was dehydrating.

The drip was in my arm by now and a doctor was squeezing the drip through me. A nurse was by my side ready with oxygen. I was lucky I was already on a side ward because of the infection in my knee.

I was later told by a doctor that I had been given the wrong antibiotic.

June, my wife, was called to come to me from the nursing home. I was now all wired up, and was taken to be treated. My temperature was still 102°. Then they put me on a catheter to record the fluid passing through my body. I thought the nurse was threading beads.

June came to me in her wheelchair and stayed until I was transferred to the RSI in Shrewsbury and put on an isolation ward to be treated.

My temperature was still 102°. I was put on a water bed with four fans around my bed to try and get it down to normal.

The nurse gave me a little yellow tablet which I still take at home and by morning the rash had gone and I was feeling much better and was put on the ward for a day then taken back to SOH.

After taking out the catheter, I was home in a week and walking on arm sticks.


Since 29th December 1994 up to 4th December 2003 I have been in hospital ten times; broken leg, six knee jobs, two heart attacks, angioplasty and chest infection.

I would like to finish on a rather sad note. Sadly my wife June passed away after a very long illness. June passed away at the Royal Shrewsbury Hospital on 18th June 2003, aged seventy-three.

June had been diagnosed with MS and Parkinson's in the early 90s but managed to get around well until she had to use a wheelchair for shopping, trips and holidays. It was around my broken leg time that she became totally wheelchair bound. In 1997 June stopped sleeping in bed and was in her wheelchair twenty-four hours a day. Every time I went into hospital June had to go into a nursing home.

My step-children all got married and drifted away. June would have liked to have gone to stay with them, or have them stay with her, but — "We can't have you Mum because we have no downstairs toilet" or "We have to go to work" (which they all did of course). But two of them lived locally and the other two lived within twenty miles of home. My own son Ian lived in Nottingham and we saw more of him than those who lived locally, and that is why we drifted apart.

June had very good carers, including Barbara Harrison, who took to her and spent extra time with her. Barbara brought her every day to see me when I was in hospital; picking her up from the nursing home and helping to get June and her wheelchair in and out of the car, she was very good.

I did manage to take her twice to the Highland Cattle Sales at Oban in Scotland when she was inbetween knee jobs. I remember quite well the last sale we went to. June wanted a black heifer and I was to bid for it with a limit of £1,000. I bid on three two-year-old heifers but they went over our £1,000 limit. What did June do when we got home? Well she said "If I cannot have a black heifer, I'll have a new carpet and dishwasher instead." That's women for you.

We had the carpet laid and I still use the dishwasher. I do all my own housework and cooking. We have a ten-roomed house, all fully furnished, so it can't be all bad.

One day I collected June with our new Corsa from the nursing home to go for the day for dinner and tea at June's cousin's at Kingsley near Stoke-on-Trent. Off we went towards Oswestry about 9.30 a.m. The road was dry and we pulled up at some traffic lights at Four Crosses behind a Land Rover and trailer. A 4x4 came and hit our car and sent us into the Land Rover and trailer. I had whiplash so could not move. June was screaming but were unable to help each other.

The lady in the Land Rover and trailer came to see whether we were badly hurt and then phoned for an ambulance. The man in the 4x4 who ran into us never came to the car to say he was sorry. He was on his way to Scotland. He worked for Wincanton Logistic and he later got fined heavily at Welshpool court.

Two ambulances arrived, one for June and one for me. I didn't know you are not allowed to carry two patients in one ambulance. The paramedics came to me first and put me in a neck brace before taking me to the RSH in Shrewsbury. June followed later in the other ambulance.

We were kept in the hospital for two or three hours before being given the all-clear. We were taken back to the nursing home but I had to pay for a taxi to take me home — twenty quid! But I did get it back later.

My battle to obtain compensation sadly lasted until June passed away. The Insurance Company originally offered only £2,000, which my insurers said was not enough; eventually they paid out £6,000.

# Contentment

We walked along the country lanes
Beneath the summer sun,
To us it seemed the world was new
Our lives had just begun.

Your eyes were like two twinkling stars
Set in a velvet sky,
Your smile was like the tiny flowers
That bowed as we passed by.

But now the country lanes are gone,
There's streets instead of flowers,
Still hand in hand we sit and dream
Of those happy carefree hours.

We've travelled through life's changing scene,
We've seen good times and bad,
Yet if we had to choose again
We'd choose the one we've had.

Now as we walk towards the light
Of everlasting day,
Bent with the load we've had to bare
With the part we've had to play.

Your smile is just as sweet as when
We wandered hand in hand,
And will be as we wander
Into the promised land.

*The above poem was written by Cyril Alcock for his wife around the time of their Diamond Wedding Anniversary — sadly she passed away in 1991. (Mr Alcock is a cousin of the author's wife.)*

## Loos at Last

At last we have Port-a-Loos on Llechwedd-Du car park and I have written a short song to the tune of Jim Reeves "Welcome to my world" to stick on the toilet door, and it sounds like this:

Welcome to our loos
Won't you come on in.
Welcome to our loos
It happens now and then.
Welcome to our loos
Leave your cares behind.
Welcome to our loos
It happens to mankind.

# The Pub With No Grub

*(Lake Vyrnwy Hotel)*

Now you've heard of the pub with no beer,
Well it could never happen around here.
But a pub with no grub
Is a bit of a snub
But it happened one night quite near.

We got ready to go out for a meal
You know how you sometimes feel.
We didn't want to go far,
So I helped June get into the car,
And to the LVH with appeal.

We were met by the staff
This was a bit of a laugh.
"We are sorry to say
No food served today.
The chef we have is a little bit naff."

So off to Llangynog we went,
The meal was money well spent.
The staff at the 'New Inn' were great,
You see we were a little bit late.
I do hope this will make them repent.

## No Loos

No loos around the lake.
Must be a big mistake.
If you wanna go for a wee,
You go behind a tree.
If you wanna go to the other,
You must go behind another.
Bring back the Port-a-Loos,
Then that would be good news.

Oh what are we to do
Without a Port-a-Loo?
If you wanna drop your pants,
Watch out for flying ants.
If you wanna go for a wee,
Watch out for the bumblebee.
Bring back the Port-a Loos,
For everyone to use.